About the Author

Josephine N. Norward is a resident of the United States and an Associate Professor of Social Work at Kean University, New Jersey. She is the daughter of one of South Africa's 1950s Drum magazine writers, the late Henry Nxumalo.

Honoring My Village

Josephine N. Norward

Honoring My Village

Olympia Publishers
London

www.olympiapublishers.com
OLYMPIA PAPERBACK EDITION

A CIP catalogue record for this title is
available from the British Library.

ISBN: 978-1-80439-330-7

This is a work of creative nonfiction. The events are portrayed to the
best of the author's memory. While all the stories in this book are true,
some names and identifying details have been changed to protect the
privacy of the people involved.

First Published in 2023

Olympia Publishers
Tallis House
2 Tallis Street
London
EC4Y 0AB

Printed in Great Britain

Dedication

I dedicate this book to my deceased parents – Henry and Florence Nxumalo, my deceased brother Henry, ex-husband Howard, daughters – Ntuthu and Mandisa, and my grandson Aasim Henry.

Acknowledgments

I thank my dearest sister Suzette for her unwavering support and encouragement in completing this book.

PREFACE

Soweto, as an acronym for southwestern townships, is a residential community composed of several townships that are eight kilometers outside of the city of Johannesburg, South Africa. It has a population of approximately a million Africans who were forced to live in this crowded segregated area, in keeping with the policies of apartheid. The writer describes 'My Village' as a metaphorical view of Soweto where she was born and raised in the late 1950s to the 1960s. The observation, description and examples cited are drawn from her own life experiences in Soweto, largely during the late 1960s to 1980, and opinions drawn from recent visits to her home country. As a native of South Africa, she spent part of her childhood in Soweto and years of her schooling in Swaziland. She draws similarities between values found in villages with those that were prevalent in Soweto. Such values are exemplified through empathy, respect, care, warmth and kindness to fellowmen. They are also encompassed under the African adage of Ubuntu.

In this book, Soweto is viewed as having a unique bond that is symbolized by a sense of affinity with one another. It is expressed through laughter to ease pain and humiliation. Humor serves as a source of self-preservation and sustainment. Care and support in times of grief and death ensures unity for residents. The return of boys as men from the 'Mountains', a traditional practice for

11

certain tribal groups following circumcision, weddings, childbirth, college graduations, are a source of pride, unity, resilience and optimism about the village's future. Faith, hope and the will to survive anchors everyone in brotherhood despite the systemic trauma and violence against each other. The resilience of this village is being celebrated for withstanding years of brutality under apartheid and remaining in solidarity with those who were exiled, while awaiting the rewards of a new order that was not to be. It is being honored for holding on to that spirit of humility, solidarity, loyalty, compassion for fellowmen and optimism. Lastly, it is being honored for serving as a laboratory for many who grew up here, to make good life choices after witnessing the villages' empowering influence.

I

HONORING MY VILLAGE

Moments of sadness, loss, wonder and laughter tend to engulf my spirit whenever I reminisce about that childhood community I left forty years ago. The exhilarating energy of my community was better felt on weekends when everyone was home tending to their household chores. For those who worked on Saturdays, theirs was a half day of work. Otherwise, that day would be devoted to fixing structural damages on the house, washing cars with stereos on, full blasts, or sitting on the front door stoop sharing a bottle of beer with a friend who happened to stop by. Thorough cleaning of a house, sprucing up a garden, baking or cooking special dishes in readiness to host friends and visiting relatives were all relegated to Saturdays and Sundays. This was a fun time for local children to get together playing in an open field, kicking soccer balls while the elders held their own private gossip sessions across a neighbor's fence. Other venues of the community served as meccas for nurturing creativity and exploration of music genre, poetry, ball room dance, and intellectual conversations. Local taverns commonly referred to as 'shebeens' also served a mixed bag role for the community, positive and negative. In the absence of places for Black entertainment, these shebeens became centers of social entertainment and intellectual discussions on world events despite the financial drains and tragedies they caused to wives and children who quite often would go without food.

The humanitarian spirit of the community was often displayed at Christmas time when neighbors exchanged gifts in the form of baked goods and cooked meals with each other. It was also customary for neighbors to drop in invited as well as to invite the entire neighborhood to share a feast in celebration of a wedding, engagement, christening or graduation. More somber moments occurred when the community experienced a death, illness or hospitalization of a member of the community. Such instances drew the community together in mourning, caring for one another and praying together. I grew up in this community surrounded by unconditional love which would often be expressed through validation messages. Such messages were a reflection of who I was to others. It was a common practice to hear teachers or neighbors expressing positive things about their students. I constantly received and internalized these positive verbal and non-verbal messages communicated by my parents, uncles, aunts, teachers and the elders of the community. As a result, I grew up self-assured. I knew I was special. I dismissed any criticisms about my looks, or my intellect. I was never intimidated by classmates who used big words to sound intellectually gifted. While I would be resentful when someone made a smart comment about acne that covered my forehead in my adolescence years, the shape of my nose or legs, I never particularly cared because my mirror shared a different picture. I liked looking at myself in the mirror. I used the mirror to practice on my smiles, grins, or how to wear a serious look. During each of my self-validation moments, I would reflect on something negative that someone had expressed about me then wonder, "What is their problem? This is good enough for me." Looking back, these were my self-aggrandizing moments which helped me to work on my sense of self, amidst negative messages from the dominant White culture.

The day I made a decision to leave my community and country after a failed marriage, bad decisions, an engagement on a rebound, Mother's death and a wrongful arrest during the political upheavals of the 1970s, was the right one. Though I carried guilt for abandoning my family my hope was to make it wherever I ended up and be in a better financial position to help my siblings and members of my extended family. I owed it to the community and family because they gave me the gift of believing in myself. My father had modeled courage to us as children. Mother on the other hand exemplified a gentle spirit of caring for one's fellowmen; compassion and empathy. As parents, they were admired by their children for raising them with tough love and for modeling hard work. Father was hardly around, covering major stories as a journalist, while Mother attended to the sick, the injured and the dying as a registered nurse with an odd work schedule. To this day, I will never forget an astonishing statement she made in her hospital bed a few days before her passing. She bestowed me with good wishes and blessings to further my education. It was during one of my visitations to her hospital ward after she had been admitted following a dizzy spell and a fall on the railway tracks while waiting for a train. As soon as she saw me, she beamed with joy. She then motioned toward her sisters who were visiting her. "This one is going to earn many, many diplomas," she said. We all laughed. However, I remained puzzled by the statement. At the time, I did not fully grasp the meaning of that statement. Moreover, I had detected a gradual mental decline in her following that accidental fall. It was only after her death that I gained an insight into her statements and held on to her words. Her wishes kept on gnawing at me, and I began to have a sense of optimism about venturing out of my little world and attempting to become a citizen of the world. I realized that Mother was giving me blessings to explore and accomplish my life's dreams. My perseverance, confidence and knowledge that my family and community were my strongest cheerleaders, were the impetus to leaving a country I loved, and the people who knowingly and unknowingly left an indelible mark on my psyche.

Given all the years I have been away from that nurturing, warm, kind and giving environment, where everyone constantly reminded me about my father's bravery to address the country's injustices, which showered every young person with compliments about their smile, attire or what would seem to be a frivolous act like picking up an item for someone that accidentally dropped it to the ground, I often wondered what exactly made my community so uniquely loving, closely bonded and tough on discipline, extremely judgmental with less tolerance for failure, antisocial and reckless behaviors. Needless to say, those were different times in comparison to today's standards. Then, it was the 1950s and 1960s. In case you wonder at the ironies of the times, all you have to do is to look around your own community and understand the dynamics of social change. Sometimes when communities and societies strive for political, economic and social change, in the process they lose a bigger piece of who they were in the past. They become a complex mix of the old and the new, with little unique character left for self-identification.

In my adulthood and as a teacher, I have since learned about the intended and unintended consequences of social policies. For those policies that are geared toward drastic social change to supposedly right past wrongs as in the case of South Africa, the ramifications were horrendous. While correcting injustices of the apartheid systems particularly the impact it had on the basic human rights of Black South Africans, on a larger scale, Black South Africans are now worse off than was ever expected. Under the current administration, their quality of life has since eroded with little investment in education, integrity in government and the pervasive greed that has permeated through every structure of society. It tears through the soul to watch the flashy TV episodes, depicting the grandiose lifestyle of young people living in high society, driving fancy cars with expensive tastes for their wines and liquor amidst the large scale of poverty-ridden communities throughout the country of all racial groups. Unfortunately, the values have changed because none of that material wealth is a substitute for a good education and upright moral values that were a thread that bound every child growing up in Soweto. Such shows only pacify the resentment that the majority feel when they look at their empty future. The selling of false and unrealistic expectations is dangerous and likely tied into money-laundering and the underground drug world which has infiltrated the South African market, turning once decent neighborhoods into hollows of people who occupy abandoned buildings that they use for drugs. Ironically, the drug lords and pushers are believed to be foreigners and the victims are by and large naïve Black South African youths. The title to Alan Paton's 1948 book, *Cry the Beloved Country* was, and is still, poignant to the social, economic and political challenges that are facing the current state of the country.

My community and neighborhood is one of several townships within the jurisdiction of Johannesburg known as Soweto, an acronym for southwestern townships.

I still talk about Soweto with passion. It is a sprawling Black township of more than a million people from different tribal groups who coexisted harmoniously. The intermarriages across tribal differences and racial differences with people from mixed racial racial groups, created a rich blending of traditions, religions and dialects unique to the community. Children of my generation who were raised in Soweto could speak mostly four dialects, Zulu, Xhosa, Sotho and Tsotsi-tal, the latter, a derivative of broken Afrikaans, a language mostly spoken by members of mixed racial communities.

Historically, Soweto became a residential community for the majority of African families legally born and raised in the urban areas of Johannesburg. When Sophia town was designated a 'Whites Only', those families moved to Orlando which would later change names to Soweto. Migrants from rural areas of South Africa who came to Johannesburg in search of work in the diamond and gold mines also found housing in Soweto's secluded 'males only' migrant hostels. Then, Soweto had a thriving middle class of physicians, nurses, social workers, teachers, small businesses, accountants, factory and service workers who had pride about their community and what it represented. As many Sowetans would attest, poverty existed but the majority of those deemed poor did not even know it because neighbors, friends, extended family members made it possible for these families to put food on the table. Besides, they carried themselves with dignity. The poverty I witnessed was never associated with criminality or any antisocial behaviors. The poor were upright people, who dragged their children to church for worship every Sunday just like every family in the neighborhood. Their children attended school regularly like every other child in the neighborhood, kept their yards clean, shined their stoops every day. Other than my mother who was very particular about her neighbors' levels of education, ordinarily, it was not easy to categorize families' economic status because families in those days were thrifty and worked very hard to ensure they had food on the table. As children, we all had meals at our neighbors' homes.

This was due to the fact that it was common practice to feed children who walked into your house no matter what the circumstances were. Perhaps signs of being poor were evidenced by those children who frequented neighbors' homes at meal times. This is what made Soweto so unique. Most of the accomplished Black South Africans of the 1980s–1990s were products of that environment. Everybody was Mama, Baba, Sisi, Bhuti and Couzy – for Mother, Father, Sister, Brother and Cousin; symbolic terms used in a family. Indeed, Soweto was a big family.

But even in a loving and caring community, Soweto's social and cultural diversity was also home to feared crime syndicates who made the community even more fascinating, despite the fear that sometimes would grip certain notorious parts of the community. Members of these syndicates were polite, well-respected 'gentlemen', debonair in looks resembling African American men of the 1960s who graced America's Ebony magazine. Though members of this syndicate group carried themselves with dignity, they could not allay rumors about their craft and association with the underground world of gangsters with roots in Alexandria and old Sophia town townships which were quite separate from the Soweto jurisdiction. Members of these groups drove in fancy foreign cars which generated even more curiosity about the source of their wealth. A word of caution in the neighborhood was, never make any innuendos in public about these 'gentlemen' because you would be strongly rebuked and at times wrestled. Any unsolicited gossip about them would be met with a stern dismissal: 'Bro? Oh no! It's totally a lie. He'd never do such a thing. People are just jealous'. My translation of that message was, 'never raise such an issue ever again'.

The real actions, symbolic of Hollywood's thrilling gangster movies mostly occurred mid-week, in broad day light, while children were in school and adults at work. One was likely to catch the real action while on sick time or having a day off. Otherwise, those who missed the action, could always rely on free post-action narrators who were readily available to relive what happened during your absence, of-course with a pinch of hyperbolic action. The only time I actually witnessed a heist, not necessarily in progress but it's get-away, with police cars in hot pursuit was at the time, I was employed by the City Council of Johannesburg as a social worker responsible for clients who lived in the central and further south parts of Soweto, commonly referred to as deep Soweto.

I was leaving a client's home when suddenly I heard the scriking noise coming from police sirens drawing louder and closer to where I was standing. I completely froze unsure if the client would let me into the house again or if I should just stand by until the commotion ceased. As I looked up the hill in the direction of the city of Johannesburg, I saw small crowds standing by the road side. In a blink of an eye, a meat truck was descending down the road at a speed close to a hundred miles per hour on a narrow street with residential homes on either side. As it passed those crowds, I could hear cheers and whistles similar to those of OJ Simpson in a Bronco making his supposedly slow, parade get-away. My mind took time to process what I was watching. As it approached my direction, I wondered to myself how safe it was to be seen. Should I turn around and pretend I was not watching? One thing for sure, I was not going to cheer this crazy, reckless driving which forced motorists to pull over as it drove by. Three police cars, one an unmarked car followed at a distance of a mile. I knew right there, the chase was history, the truck was gone. As expected, when I got home, the free narrators were eager to relate every piece of the action, with a touch of suppositions about possible destinations and benefactors of that meat truck. Subsequent to that dramatic chase, each time I would walk past butcher stores in the community, I often wondered who actually ended up benefitting from that hold-up of a meat truck. Most likely, a few butchers got a stake of that meat at a reasonable price. So was the thrill of my community.

Oppression does a lot of harm to the human spirit. It eats away at the tenets that were once inculcated to children at a young age, so as to guide them toward leading a moral life. It creates confusion, contradictions and desperation to anyone in pursuit of living a meaningful and an honest life. People grow up with good intentions but then are indirectly corrupted by prevailing systems of injustice. While some may view the latter as a lousy excuse, it actually is a valid area for analyzing the contextual nature of human behavior in terms of misconceptions that prevail about Black South Africans. Not many White South Africans have an understanding of how corrosive that system was and still is to Black South Africans. Perhaps those who hired live-in maids had a different and more compassionate understanding of the effects it had on their lives. Perhaps, they also felt they had little influence to change that system.

The basis for many disparities in South Africa was the racial classification of the population. Of importance to this discussion was the disparities in education, employment, wages and salaries across South Africa's system of racial classification. This system afforded all members of the White race to be first-class citizens; the privileged group, followed by Asian (Indians, Chinese), then Coloreds (members of mixed races) and lastly Blacks. Needless to say, the White population enjoyed a privileged lifestyle, as did the other racial groups. Blacks survived on a pittance salaries compared to the other groups. With that came self-discipline and frugality because for Black people, working over-time and taking a second job was unheard of. One held on to one's job for life because if one were to lose it the rippling effect, and the impact it had on others, was significant. To augment those poor wages and salaries, there were people who resorted to stealing from their own places of employment so as to sell stolen merchandise in Soweto. The trend then was to steal and sell brand new tires and plush car seat covers. Though transistor radios were also popular, the drawback was the difficulty of getting a license for a stolen radio to prove one was a legitimate owner. Not being able to produce a license of ownership when inspections were conducted, meant paying high fees in excess of the value of the radio. Basically, the practice was, if one needed a new tire, one had to reach out to those who carried such merchandise and place an order. Other items which were sold were hand-bags, music records, adult and children's clothing. These activities took place on Saturdays, a day after weekly earners were paid, and at the end of the month. The sellers would walk door to door peddling their stolen merchandise. In those days, police officers were never seen in the neighborhood. Therefore, there was never a fear of being arrested on the part of these peddlers. With time and sophistication in the art of stealing, stealing fancy and foreign made cars, became a popular trend. Rarely would such cars be stolen from residents. They would be stolen from the suburbs. Also, the stealing of luxury cars was rarely for local sales but for foreign countries. They would be driven across the borders of South Africa to other African countries.

Soweto became a center for international tourist attractions. It was common to see luxury tourists' bus, or two or three driving in a convoy around Soweto – sometimes escorted by police cars. I often saw these buses early in the morning before lunch time, while making my rounds in the community as a social worker, visiting my clients. The passengers were White. The buses made frequent stops to take photos of residential houses and historic sites. Only recently, they have been spending time to take lunch at local restaurants. Such scenes often puzzled me. I found a number of the laws that were the basis of the apartheid system to be full of contradictory messages to the outside world. For example, White people were barred from visiting Soweto because it was deemed dangerous and unsafe. Also, Black South Africans were often described as lazy, violent and not to be trusted. Yet, those very Black maids raised White children while parents were at work, took care of the homes, ran errands, slept in their maid quarters and only left one day a week, on their day off. Now buses full of foreign White people were touring Soweto not afraid of the supposedly violent Black people? Questions raised by regular Sowetans were, 'is the curiosity about Soweto negative or positive? Are these White foreigners on some kind of fact-finding mission for the United Nations or to perhaps attest to the workings of the apartheid regime? Was my community some kind of an amusement park? Was it because we were caged, contained, with limited freedom of movement and freedom of speech? Were these some types of comparisons between what had been done to First Nations people.' Perhaps all those mixed feelings were a direct result of the apartheid regime's portrayal of who we were as a community. I often wondered if those tourists were also accustomed to making similar tours of their own countries' ghettos places like Harlem, the Bronx, Baltimore, Brixton, Hackney, Lambeth or what is referred to as Muslim ghettos in Antwerp, Molenbeek in Belgium and Paris? This fascination with Soweto seemed to intensify in the post-apartheid era. Also troubling was the notion that Soweto was commonly referred to as a ghetto during the years I lived there in the 1950s through the 1980s. Understandably, it does fit into parts of the definition that describes a ghetto as, 'part of a city, mainly a slum area occupied by a minority group, isolated and segregated'. Similar areas are all over the United States but interestingly, none of them are referred to as ghettos. Despite the negative perceptions, Soweto took pride in its surroundings composed of a mixture of fancy large homes with two level Spanish-style architecture or modern style ranch houses and well-manicured, brick-fenced yards. Such homes still grace large pockets of Soweto's streets. Owned by the community's physicians, businessmen, tavern owners, teachers, lawyers, regular factory workers, these homes were a great indicator that every human being who worked hard, had the same aspirations as the White suburbanites to accomplish a decent standard of living and that they could actually have such comfort. Homes in Soweto were a mixture of structures from those designed by the government's local authority agencies such as the City Council of Johannesburg to those torn down by private individuals and redesigned to suit their tastes. In essence, a number of individuals replaced those City Council match box dwellings consisting of two-bedrooms, a kitchen, living room, pantry and no inside bathroom nor an inside toilet, with bigger and decent houses. Whenever I think about the architects of apartheid, I shudder. Obviously, to them, we were not humans that were deserving of having an inside lavatory in these homes, but an outhouse. We were not human enough to deserve to have a bathroom in these homes for taking a shower or a bath. Yet, the poorest White families lived in decent homes. It appears most Black South Africans in Soweto knew this because every family had a relative who worked as a domestic worker for poor White families, and out of curiosity made sure to visit their relatives to see how these people lived. Given those types of disparities, Black families who could afford it and those who could not afford it made necessary changes to accommodate their needs and to break the monotonous pattern of housing in Soweto. In my eight years of working as a social worker in Soweto, doing home visits, I would be taken aback by the cleanliness of most of those homes I visited that housed poor families. Based on those experiences, I knew that being poor was not equivalent to being lazy because my clients' homes in Soweto were spotlessly clean. Though not professionally endorsed to do so, quite often I accepted an offer for tea.

I dare say Soweto has since changed. Today it is likely to be twice the size of its original population with signs of abject poverty all around, and fewer middle-class families. Everywhere one turns there are squatter camps. In single resident's homes, there are squatters in the backyards. The rationale I often get is that the majority of people are unemployed so they take in illegal immigrants from Mozambique, Zimbabwe etc. to shack in their backyards in exchange for monthly rent. The crowding and unsanitary conditions of this arrangement leave much to be desired. There is another layer to this problem involving corruption in Soweto's housing market. Under South Africa's Reconstruction and Development program (RDP) that was instituted by Nelson Mandela to increase affordable housing, nowadays, these houses are purchased by people for profit making purposes under the real estate market. People with money get what has become the biggest government scam of offering people 'business tenders' with little or no accountability, to ensure that the product or service has been adequately delivered.

Unemployment in the Southern African region has forced many people to migrate to South Africa. This has presented a huge problem for a country still trying to deal with historical injustices. The number of unskilled laborers descending on South Africa from neighboring African countries has been ongoing for the past twenty years. Sadly, it has indirectly pitted Black South Africans against immigrants who are mostly preferred in today's hiring practices for domestic work and other industries. While this practice is commonly viewed as a blatant exploitation of immigrants, employers view it differently. Their reasoning is that Black South Africans are too selective and want more money. Also, they feel they are entitled to benefit somehow from past injustices. To be fair, this is not a practice confined to White employers only. Black employers are doing the same thing in that their preference is to hire immigrants rather than their own people. This practice has numerous complexities involved. One is the fact that the government, which basically is the ANC, is the largest employer of Black South Africans. As a result, those who can afford to hire anyone are deemed to represent a corrupt government and because of the mistrust, they walk a fine line with the general public. In essence, they are afraid to bring Black South Africans into their homes by hiring them. Secondly, the resentment in the Black community over members of the ANC and the entire government has been percolating for years. The ANC is blamed by a majority of Black South Africans for their failures to deliver what they had promised, years ago. The general perception has always been that the ANC leveraged with those African governments who offered them refuge while they were in exile. In return, they had to 'pay back' post-apartheid by opening their borders for all Africans seeking refuge in South Africa, for whatever reasons. Lastly, the ills facing today's communities of South Africa in the form of drugs, human trafficking, raping of children and femicide are associated with immigrants.

When I left South Africa, Soweto was a quiet, deserted place during week days because every child would be in school and every able-bodied adult at work. In other words, life in Soweto during week days was far different from the care-free, leisurely lifestyle of the week-ends. Typically, on weekends, almost every house had their stereos blowing loud with music while others threw parties or held traditional gatherings. Weekends were days to hang-out in whatever form. Hence, I was taken aback in 2008 on a visit home after my brother's death. I was staying at a cousin's place in the suburbs of Johannesburg and took a ride to Soweto for the weekend. On my way back the following Monday, a friend offered me a ride to take me back to the suburbs. As we rode through Diep Kloof, another section of Soweto, I was stunned by the number of people casually roaming the streets on a weekday. As I turned my head, at all angles, I was totally in disbelief seeing all these people. I turned toward my friend who was driving, and I asked her, "What time is it?"

She said, "Oh, it is a quarter to twelve, why?"

I said, "It is a Monday and during this time of the day, children are usually in schools and adults at work." She laughed and knew what I was referring to. She went on to tell me just how bad the situation was after the closures of garment factories and the influx of cheap Chinese products into the market. She went on to decry the irony of South Africa's struggling economy that could not hire its own youths at a time when it was supposed to be enjoying majority rule following the 1990s victory of the most powerful political party of the ANC. While some believe the current government carries the economic and social burdens and failures of the apartheid regime, others point a finger at the current ruling party. Others hold on to a wide speculation which contends that when the White regime ended they funneled all of South Africa's wealth offshore. While this might be quite a stretch, it is possible. However, is it not enough to explain the country's disastrous economic failures amidst wide-spread mismanagement. When one listens to such speculations, then a counter question is how did these few members of the ANC become billionaires over night? There is so much corruption, ineptitude, entitlement, a lack of empathy, cronyism and failures to govern to the extent that lawlessness reigns by the hour. Almost every South African complains about the presence of Nigerians in the country and their unsavory business practices

28

that are generally viewed as despicable. Despite the public's concerns, they have found a home in South Africa and are flourishing while the ANC has turned a blind eye to the menace they have caused in the country. One has to wonder, what's in it for those who are governing the country. What deals do they have with top officials of the ANC to engage in their activities so boldly, and rent out most of the White owned apartment buildings in Hillbrow that were abandoned by their owners, as if they were the rightful landowners? While trying to understand that part of an argument, then there's the issue of neighboring countries who have exerted their own economic burdens on South Africa. No country would allow such an unprecedent surge of unskilled immigrants and their families to their country without imposing any penalties. I have watched so many borders patrol shows on DANGER TV that cover immigration practices and their stringent approaches to enforcing immigration policies on air, land and sea. I often wonder why South Africa does not take a page to learn from them. From Mozambique, Zimbabwe, Pakistan, Nigeria to name a few, illegal immigrants have been descending on South Africa in unprecedent ways in the last ten years, accompanied by white-collar criminals, and the underground criminals who have found a haven for their criminal activities in South Africa. Unfortunately, politicians have not been spared of being actively involved in such practices. A case in point is that of a former president's implication in one of South Africa's notorious racketeering and money-laundering schemes involving arms deals with foreign countries.

As a social worker in South Africa in the 1970s, I can recall that the most pervasive drug of choice that was destroying Black people in South Africa was alcohol. At that time, glue-sniffing by teenage runaways who slept under bridges or sewer pipes was also prevalent. Any other drug was unheard of at least to regular folks. This however changed as former South African who had lived abroad and were users returned back home. In addition, around that time, Nigerians were believed to have begun peddling a potent drug known as Mandrax. Whereas in earlier days, regular folks could not afford such drugs like cocaine, in the current era of South Africa there are numerous illegal drugs that are destroying fellow brothers and sisters. When one listens to the description of some of the concoctions that are used for these drugs one wonders if, unconsciously, the users are trying to kill themselves rather than wake up to the emptiness of their lives with no food, home, family nor expectations of a brighter future. My own family dealt with a family member who was and still is literally lost in that world of drugs, with no hope of ever making it through recovery. The other dilemma facing South Africans is how to deal with family members who are caught up in the drug culture because it is new to most people in South Africa. Other countries had dealt with heroin and all kinds of drugs. I am inclined to think South Africans were immune to them simply because borders were sealed with restrictive traveling outside the country. Consequently, in the absence of drug problems, there was no treatment other than Alcoholics Anonymous. Again, for anyone who knew the oppressive system of apartheid that robbed people of the rights to lead decent and fulfilling lives, socially, emotionally, economically and politically for Black people, taverns or shebeens provided meaningful outlets to congregate for intellectually stimulating conversation which involved social and political discourse over alcohol. Hence, there was an unsaid rationale for visiting these shebeens to spend days imbibing in alcohol because they served a meaningful purpose, with little attention paid to the negative ramifications on individuals, family and community's well-being.

II

PRIDE IN MY BI-TRIBAL UPBRINGING

Against this backdrop of my community is the family that served as the bedrock of my upbringing. As a product of a bi-tribal union, I celebrate my Xhosa and Zulu linage with pride. I was raised by working parents, a journalist and a registered nurse. My maternal grandmother Lily, better known as Momkhulu, lived with my family. She was a helper who took care of the five children. She also was the caretaker of my home, while my parents worked long hours. Grandma Lily cooked, took care of our laundry, cleaned the house, walked my siblings and I to school, tucked us in bed at night, taught us how to pray before we went to bed and assured us how we were special and loved by, our parents. Reciting night prayers and comforting us when we were sick, are some of the fondest memories of her presence in my life. As children, we learned how to speak Xhosa from her. However, when we used my father's dialect, Zulu, she would respond in Xhosa. She never addressed my father in Zulu, only in Xhosa. She had this passive-aggressiveness about her that often made my father oblige and respond likewise. Though it was never verbally addressed, as children, we surmised Xhosa was the preferred medium of communication in our family. Looking back, the stereotyping of tribal groups was prevalent as well. As a child, I grew up hearing all kinds of stereotypes from adults mainly about Xhosas and Zulus. Xhosas were thought to be

31

smart, arrogant and cunning to the extent that one had to take anything they promised with a pinch of salt. Based on these stereotypes, Xhosas were thought to be very well educated. On the other hand, Zulus were considered polite, humble, honest yet stubborn and quick to get into a fight. Sotho were another popular tribal group in Soweto. They were viewed as amiable, easily getting along with everyone. Nothing negative was, to my knowledge, said about them. Overall, in Soweto, these stereotypes were meaningless as intermarriages between the tribes were prevalent.

Grandma Lily had a willowy stature. At six feet and thin, she towered over my father's height of five foot six. She was a busy-bee. Rarely would one find her sitting or wondering aimlessly. In her earlier years, she worked as a domestic worker for Jewish families in the suburbs of Johannesburg. Hence, from the time she woke up, she would multi-task until bedtime. I enjoyed keeping pace with her, running around, asking her all kinds of questions. At six years old, I had a limited English vocabulary but one of the first words I learned from her was 'nuisance'. Whenever I asked her questions, she would swing around saying, "Joey, you are becoming a nuisance. Go and play with your siblings." But I was drawn to her energy and mood swings. She finally realized the only way she could contain me would be to keep me busy and engage me in whatever activities she was doing. As a result, I learned that flour was the only common ingredient for making bread, cakes, scones, puddings and tarts otherwise, each had its own unique ingredients, with precise measurements. These were special moments with Grandma Lily. Whatever she was baking, I would be right there on call, running between the pantry and the kitchen to pick up an item she needed, climbing on chairs to reach for items that were beyond my reach. I learned a lot from her by observing how each task was performed with precision, with little room for error. This was the beginning of my love for cooking, baking, sewing, cleaning, ironing and knitting.

A day I would never forget was when she asked me to reach out for a bottle of vinegar from the pantry. I told her I could not because it was rather too high on the shelf. She zipped past me, picked up a bottle, used it, placed it back on the shelf and dished out lunch for me and my siblings. The five of us sat down to eat. Shortly thereafter, we looked at each other and in unison, we ran to a drain outside the house, spitting the food, rinsing mouths and complaining, "Grandma, there's soap in the food!"

She yelled back, "Your mother spoiled you. Sit down and eat that food."

As we protested, she yelled louder and louder until a neighbor could over-hear the fracas. The neighbor walked over to our yard and asked, "Lily, what is the problem?"

She responded, "Tutu's children are spoiled. They need a spanking." Meanwhile we were chattering amongst ourselves disputing what she was saying. As the neighbor overheard what we were saying about the taste of soap in our food, she took a spoon to taste it, turned to my grandmother shaking her head in disbelief and dashed to spit the food and rinse her mouth. She calmly asked Grandma what she had added to the curried dish she had cooked. Grandma quickly reached for the same bottle she had picked earlier from the pantry. It turned out to be a liquid starch which she often used when ironing her daughter's uniform. It was obvious that Grandma was embarrassed. From that point on, we rarely spoke about that incident because we never wanted to hear her daughter yelling at her or accusing her of endangering her children nor did we want my father asking her to leave. As her grandchildren, we were too attached and loyal to her. We also knew we were her favorite grandchildren. Though she had her property in old Pimville, a slum area close to Kliptown, she enjoyed our company, and loved being at my parents' place. One thing I so vividly remember about her were her mood swings. I would notice this side of her vacillating from being in a good mood playing around with us one minute, then the next minute engulfed in a gloomy cloud. At that age, I did not know what it was or how to describe it. For instance, if either of my parents returned from work and asked her about her day, she would simply look at them, not say a word or walk away. She would maintain that silence until she went to bed and if we tried to play with her she would completely ignore us. At other times, she would exchange words with her daughter. Between mother and daughter, one could never tell who started the arguments. One thing was for sure; my father, with his calm nature, became the mediator. At times, Grandma took it hard. When that happened, she would wait until both my parents left for work the following day, then get us ready, not to go to school but for a trip by bus to her place in Pimville. A small suitcase would be packed for the trip. Quite often, such days would coincide with her pension day. Needless to say, going to Pimville for us meant days full of fun. We did not have to go to school. After our morning porridge, we would run to a store on the corner in the company of our cousins who were much older than us. Grandma's pension day was everyone else's spending day. All the things we could not have at my parents' house were possible at Grandma's place. We would have all kinds of candy, chewing gum, fish and chips and fat cakes. We played in muddy streets, tagged along behind

34

Grandma to check on her two cows and watched as the man at this run-down fenced area where the cows were kept would start milking them. We visited the entire side of my mother's family, our aunts, uncles and cousins. This was a huge family. Based on family accounts, Grandma had seven children from her first husband, and five from the second husband, with Mother being the last born. By her looks, and based on the accounts of older cousins, Grandma was part of the Cape Malay racially mixed group. Regretfully, this part of my family history was rarely shared. Two maternal uncles who were twins, were a spitting image of Grandma with dark non-African features and dark straight hair. Interestingly, they would always have their heads covered, Grandma always covered herself in a head scarf, and my uncles always had hats on. In my adulthood, I often wondered if it was to conceal their hair texture and to protect themselves from violating the nebulous racial classification laws of South Africa? Was it due to South Africa's racial classification which paid much credence to physical features and genealogical background? These were tough and uncomfortable questions to raise to Grandma or Mother. Besides, I was too young at the time. Most of these puzzling questions only came to me in my early adulthood. However even in my adulthood before Mother passed away, they were never openly discussed.

Grandma Lily's death signified a very sad moment for me. This was a realization for me about life that those you love do depart from this earth, and you never get to see or touch them ever again. As a child, you are left alone with your thoughts to create a reality out of something so unreal. Prior to her death, my reality was that everyone wakes up from a sleep. No one had ever talked or explained anything about a prolonged sleep such as death.

It was on a very busy Saturday night and Grandma had been busy all day cleaning the house, baking and hosting a number of guests who were dropping in to pray, and extend words of fellowship after my father, a World War II veteran had experienced and 'recovered' from what is today referred to as post-traumatic stress disorder. No one understood the disorder at the time just that it was a 'mental illness'. At the same time, there were members of a religious sect in the community who viewed it as a possession by evil spirits. However, to us as children, our dad was simply sick and not available to us emotionally. Now that he had recovered and was back at work, it was a joyous time for us. The family had reasons to have a two-day celebration. On that Saturday evening, Grandma said she needed to take a nap and left me, my siblings, Mother and our guests in our favorite part of the house, the kitchen. Since we were not used to being out of her sight, my siblings and I decided to go follow her later on and wake her up. Her bedroom was our bedroom. We walked in, climbed on her high, wide and comfortable bed and began fanning her. I cannot recall if she had asked to be fanned for air or we surmised it was too warm in the room. Moreover, she was tired and fanning her for air would be comfortable. Whatever the sequence of events was, Grandma would not wake up. We stomped, jumped on the bed, she would not wake up. My memory gets very blurred as to what followed. All I remember was my mother's petrifying screams; "Ma! Ma! Don't leave me." Looking back, at that moment, I witnessed for the first time my mother's vulnerability, her losing her anchor at such a delicate time. She was on maternity leave for her fifth child. Her husband had just recovered from PTSD. She was so used to her support system; her mother. Now she was all alone with no help to care for her five children. Grandma had literally raised me and my sibling while our parents pursued their respective demanding careers. Grandma Lily's death signaled the end of the jolly rides, back and forth between her house, my mother's side of the family and ours. It strongly affected my mother's emotional state.

The following year, another tragedy befell my family while we were still grieving grandmother's sudden death. The brutal murder of my father while on an assignment as a journalist shook the core of my innocence, my sense of safety and security. Losing a father and watching my mother go through another period of darkness, as she helplessly mourned the death of her husband pushed my family through a difficult phase. As children, my siblings and I had no idea of what his death meant to others. We had been sheltered from the real world and had no clue of the stories he covered and their significance to the rest of the community, and the country. Though my family always had monthly copies of the magazine DRUM and my father would read child-friendly stories to us, for the most part, some of the material was beyond our comprehension as children. It is likely that my older sister who enjoyed reading had a better understanding of the content that he covered in his stories. All the same, it was bewildering to know there were people out there who conspired to end his life in such a brutal manner. His death significantly altered the core of my family's foundation. He was murdered on New Year's Eve and I turned eight years old, that following January. At eight years old, I became aware of what I recognize today as my mother going through depression. At the time, she was also nursing a nine-month-old baby, my sister. Most likely she was also going through post-partum depression. Emotionally, she was getting detached from us, particularly from the baby. I recall times when I would check on her and be asked to take the baby with me. I would carry the baby on my back while completing house chores and because I was still a child, I would also take the baby with me to go play outside.

The strain of the ensuing criminal trial regarding my father's murder, and the controversy surrounding the killers who were hired, was too painful for my mother to endure. Luckily, the presence and support of family members and friends made a huge difference in knowing that she was not alone. Financially, the family went through tough times since Mother was still on maternity leave. Financial support from my father's employer, from family members and friends sustained us. God's mercy had prevailed because there were days when Mother was visibly concerned about our next meal. I came to witness the resilience of the human spirit as my mother pulled herself out of the doldrums. She arranged for the care of the two younger siblings and registered for a second certification in nursing at the Pietermaritzburg nursing institution, so she could be able to take care of all five of us. A paternal uncle who taught at a boarding school in Natal took two of my siblings with him and I was sent to a Catholic boarding school in Swaziland; a neighboring country of South Africa. A distant paternal aunt offered to house sit and care for my two younger siblings pending Mother's return. These arrangements allowed Mother to complete her training and return to work as a registered nurse. During her absence, she maintained regular contacts with us, sending letters and photos. From her photos, she looked well-adjusted and resolved. This was true of her demeanor when she returned. Mother was bubbly, optimistic, warm, attentive, engaging and as usual she enjoyed a good laugh. She was able to reconstruct the fiber that bonded us as a family. Upon her return, a sense of normalcy was restored.

Regular visits from paternal family members coming from the countryside and those from our maternal family's side, added so much joy to our lives. They were a source of comfort, validating who I was and where I stood in the scheme of things. They renewed and solidified my faith in what I viewed as a unified family.

A shift in my world view began when I entered St. Joseph's Catholic boarding school which was situated in the outskirts of the city of Manzini, in Swaziland. Then, Swaziland was one of the three British Protectorates in Southern Africa. They were known for their comparatively high standard of education in comparison to South Africa' s system of Bantu education. It is here where I learned how to pray the rosary, recite the catechism, confess my sins in thought, words and deeds. I got to know that my guardian angel was constantly besides me protecting and guiding me. I took these teaching in literal terms. Anything I wanted I prayed to God for. I prayed for my father's soul, my grandma's soul and those of all the relatives who had left us so they could rest in peace. I prayed to God to grant my mother the strength to heal, to be courageous to shoulder the burden of caring for five children. In addition to knowing and believing in a higher power, I learned self-discipline, hard-work, to share and to respect others.

III

THE INTRICACIES OF FAMILY

Being away from home, living in the institutional setting of a boarding school which was far different from a home setting, offered me an opportunity to appreciate my family even more. It opened up my eyes to the reality of death. I began to recognize that the world was unsafe, uncertain and not as dependable as I had thought. It certainly was not like my family. This period also allowed me to reflect more about my extended families' background, both on my mother's side and father's side. It was during those moments that I attempted to reconstruct my mother's side of the family based on my older cousins' accounts. For instance, one of her brothers who actually resembled her, lived very close to our family but because he had passed as a member of a racially mixed group, his residential area was designated for racially mixed groups only. Africans could not occupy a resident there legally. However, Uncle Mxhosa had married a woman from a racially mixed group, Aunt Kitty and raised his children as coloreds in this neighboring town of Newclare. Needless to say, there were infrequent interactions with Uncle Mxhosa's family. On rare occasions, he would bring his family to our home in Soweto for a Sunday-afternoon visit. While my mother and her brother would be enjoying the visit, reminiscing about their past, Aunt Kitty did her best to be sociable. However, fellowship with our cousins was extremely awkward. Much as we were related by blood, the strain between us as cousins was obvious. We were separated by South Africa's race classification. My cousins were considered 'coloreds' and grew up knowing they were a social class above their African cousins, therefore they were better compared to us. This was typical of so many other families because 'social passing' was a common practice and people did it to take advantage of a better socio-economic status. In essence, Uncle Mxhosa seemed very much detached from his side of the family. The last time I saw him was in the early 1970 during a hospital visit to see him with my mother. He had been admitted to Edendale hospital, located outside Johannesburg in the city of Germiston. The day of our visit, we were directed to his ward. As we walked in, Uncle Mxhosa immediately noticed his sister who was dressed in her nursing uniform. When he saw us, he motioned to us, smiling, proudly announcing to fellow patients, "This is my sister." Frankly, I do not recall him mentioning who I was. However, I do recall asking myself if those patients thought maybe I was my mother's maid. Our visit turned out to be the best thing to have happened for them. I sat there by the foot of his bed admiring the warmth they exuded toward each other. It was touching to witness the love, pain and perhaps regrets that the two harbored. Uncle Mxhosa looked visibly frail, emaciated and very sick. He was trying to prolong the visit but I could tell the talking was putting a strain on his shallow voice. As we bid our fare-wells, the separation became very emotional. Once Mother and I got to the car, I shared my earlier observation with her about the colored patients in that ward. I told her that most likely, they wondered if and how we were related to Uncle Mxhosa since I was visibly African. Could it be that they thought I was her maid? She looked at me bemused and broke into her unrestrained, hearty laughter, saying, "Don't be silly," and that signaled the end of our conversation about the visit.

Ndlambe is a second uncle who frequently stopped by our home. His visits were enroute to 'somewhere'. He was lanky, more so from starvation, with Grandma's tall, willowy height. Of all of his siblings, he was the only one who fondly referred to his sister as Balakazi, Mother's Xhosa name. From his physical disposition, one could tell he was leading a tough life. His poor hygiene, torn and greasy dusk coat which he often wore made my mother cringe each time she saw him. Yet to me and my siblings, he was fun to be around. Every time we spotted him approaching the open field which led to my home, we would run toward the house jubilantly announcing, 'Uncle Ndlambe is coming'. My sister would put water on the stove for tea, while I pulled out a mug, a saucer and a small plate for bread because we knew he would be starving. By that time, Uncle Ndlambe would be by the back door, walking toward his sister to greet her, "Molo Balakazi." Seemingly annoyed at him or embarrassed, Mother would immediately block his entrance to the kitchen door, and direct us to pull a small bunk for him to sit under a shady peach tree in the backyard. As we excitedly prepared a meal of hot tea and bread, Mother would walk toward us, ordering us to use a separate mug and plates. She could not hide her annoyance at us. We would respectfully do as directed, walk out of the house with a tray for Uncle Ndlambe. Sitting next to him and watching as he ate, we would ask him questions: "Where are you going?"

Once he finished, he would ask for a second helping while listening to his one-line sad story of losing his 'particulars' and going 'somewhere' to find them. On these occasions, once he felt nourished, he would abruptly leave and we would be left confused, sad, and troubled by our mother's reaction toward him. This would be the pattern each time he came to visit. On one occasion, either my older sister or I wanted to know from Mother what exactly happened to Uncle Ndlambe. Was he sick? What led to his unconventional life-style? He amused us so much with his words. He often uttered a profound Xhosa idiom, 'ndiphila ubomi bentaka', meaning 'I lead the life of a bird,' a very loaded, puzzling and cynical saying. Each time we remember his expressions like, 'my particulars,' 'ndiphila ubomi bentaka', we would break out in laughter. However, Mother's look would admonish us and put a stop to it. One day, we learned from Mother that her brother was once a successful tennis player, a bright young man who ruined his life. I guess at the time, that was all we needed to know. We never asked how.

Uncle Ben who appeared much older than the twins, would make sporadic visits to my family while Grandma was still alive. There was a shady side to him which was never openly discussed. Supposedly he had a family in Sophia town. He was a 'candy uncle' and would give us five shillings every time he came for a visit. After my father's death, he moved in with us for a brief time. Based on our understanding as children, his wife Mildred was a live-in domestic worker who only visited him on her day offs. However, from the grapevine, our older cousins described the relationship differently. His witty banter about life in Sophia town and stories about his involvement with mobsters made us wonder why Mother would let him move in with us. At the same time, he would contradict himself, claiming he was on the run for 'stealing' from them.

Each time we asked Mother what Uncle Ben actually did, she would tell us, "He's a wonderer. You will never get the truth from him." He drove a truck which was always parked in the back alley not at the front of the house. He strongly believed he was being followed by mobsters every night on his way home from work, hence parking the truck in the back-alley was to protect himself. His stories were bizarre and scary. Full of tricks, he would hide money, ask us to find it, turn real paper money to regular paper or to a spade card. He liked driving his truck without lights at night when approaching the alley way, then make us believe he was being followed by the mobsters. At times, he would sneak up on us at night as the boogieman. Because of his towering stature, we would be petrified and have difficulty going to sleep. Uncle Ben had a transistor radio but did not have a license for it. At the time, every house in the township with a transistor radio had to produce a license for the inspectors whenever they conducted house to house routine checks. One of his trickers was to hide this transistor radio inside the oven of the stove, before leaving for work. Though he reminded us over and over never to divulge to the inspectors we had a radio, he still did not trust us. One day, he forgot to pull the radio out of the oven before preparing a fire for cooking our supper. When we returned home from playing outside, we smelled something burning. While contemplating where the smell could be coming from, we heard this loud blast coming from the oven area of the stove. By the time Uncle Ben realized he had burnt his precious transistor radio, it was too late. Toxic fumes were coming out of the oven with a smell of burning rubber. We spent the night at a neighbor's house while Uncle Ben aired and cleaned the house. The fall out with his sister, led to his abrupt departure.

Through these fragmented experiences, I came to realize that my mother was a jewel to her family. She was revered as the youngest sister who uplifted herself, first by becoming an elementary school teacher, a nurse practitioner and a midwife. Lastly, marrying a man so driven by a passion to unfold his country's system of injustices earned her respect and admiration. By her siblings' standard, she had done well for herself. After her husband's untimely death, she proved to be a formidable woman. Single-handedly, she maintained a decent standard of living for us and provided opportunities for us to elevate ourselves through education. Though widowed at the young age of thirty-two with several suitors interested in marrying her and taking care of her five children she remained a widower until her death in 1978. She was a beautiful, warm-hearted and well-poised woman who always reminded her children, particularly her four girls to emulate her style, being soft-spoken, polite and working hard. She was a 'particular individual', protective, content and selective. Her life centered around her work and her children. If her day off fell on a Sunday, she would go to church, rush home to cook a Sunday dinner, spend an afternoon on the front stoop chatting, reconnecting with neighbors and getting the latest township gossip. Since our home was home to frequent unannounced visitations by family members, their presence brightened her spirits. I admired everything about my mother. Her warm spirit, honesty, forgiving, optimism and ability to negotiate tough periods of her children's development into young adults, it was a source of reassurance that if we were to become parents, we had a role model, and will do well. She gave us a strong foundation to use and pass it on for future generations. She was my star. Every minute I think of her, I visualize her smile and smile back at her.

My father was a member of the Zulu clan. Zulus are commonly

referred to as warriors after the Zulu king Shaka who led a victorious fight against British invasion in Zululand. He came from a village named Kwa Xolo near Port Shepstone, in the south coast of Zululand. My father's family were kind, authentic, humble, trustworthy and independent people who embraced the African adage of Ubuntu. They supported each other wherever they were. Their clan, which was spread across the country sides of Natal, Swaziland, Zimbabwe, Transvaal and parts of Soweto, always supported each other. One of the beauties of my culture is that when you shared the same surname with people not known to you or the larger family, the elders were able to draw a genealogical linkage to validate the blood relationship. Hence growing up, I had many cousins. Frankly how we were related was of least importance. Of high value was the love we shared, the support we gave each other in good times, bad times, and the spirit of fellowship in breaking bread together several times each year. Every family event was special because the elders would sit around a bonfire enjoying Bantu beers, sharing folklore about growing up Kwa Xolo. These were memorable events. The pride in who we were and of our culture was reinforced through such gatherings. As children, we always looked forward to them. From such gatherings, I grew up knowing that our father became an orphan in his teenage years. His father fell from a cliff to his death. As the eldest of four children, he had to take care of his siblings. Reportedly, his only sister passed away during their childhood years. Their paternal uncle who lived in the same village took over the responsibility of raising his brother's children.

With a knack for writing, my father dabbled in poetry and short stories. The destitution and tough existence in the village, drove him to the big lights of the city of Johannesburg. He was hired as a boiler and later enlisted with the South African national defense force. Based on archived records, during World War II, he served in the native military corps from October twentieth, 1941 to September eighteenth, 1945. Upon his return, he met and married my mother. Together they created a home for everyone who wanted to visit, have an extended stay or make our home a base in the city, away from the village, while exploring better opportunities. Some of my father's family already had jobs in the city.

A first cousin to my father, Uncle George was a school teacher at a boarding school in Natal. He spent most of his school vacations with us. Amongst his many talents, he was also a carpenter. His projects included building kitchen cabinets, fixing wardrobe shelves, doors or painting our home. As a musician, he would walk around the house whistling or humming some of the most beautiful, unheard-of tunes, teaching our only brother how to play a piano. He strongly shaped our interest and love of music. To this day, my older sister and I reminisce about happy days when family members gathered around the piano for sing-alongs with Uncle George playing or Uncle Lolo, a distant relative of my mother. Uncle George was a man of few words and most of his quiet times were spent reading. He was my mother's favorite brother-in-law. At every meal time, she made sure the table was set for Uncle George's breakfast, lunch or dinner. As I became mature and able to read and understand people's behaviors, I surmised that there was a side of him that was passive-aggressive. For instance, if it took time to let him know breakfast was served and he found it cold, he would walk away and not alert you. By the time you find out, he would either have stepped out of the house or started working on his projects.

Hearing him laugh was a rarity and when it happened, my siblings and I would race for the door, pushing each other to find his location. Once inside the house, we would simply stand there sheepishly, musing in disbelief. On such occasions, Uncle George would either have company from his teacher friends, his sister, or other members of his family.

He resembled my father in many ways. His even-keeled temperament, love of solitude, being an avid reader and most of all a musician reminded me of my father. His impact on my older sister and younger brother's upbringing is unmeasurable. He truly was a surrogate father. He is the paternal uncle who took my two siblings under his guardianship when attending school in Natal. His commitment to his brother's family was never interrupted by his subsequent marriage and move to Swaziland. He is the uncle who spearheaded my move to a boarding school in Manzini, Swaziland where he continued his role as a surrogate father to me. His wife, Aunt Beauty was the friend you found in a parent. She was tough on discipline but did it with diplomacy.

Aunt Agnes, the older sister to Uncle George was also a fixture in my home and had a profound impact on our upbringing. A spiritual, gentle and genuinely warm person, she made us feel very special. The minute she walked into the house, she would call out our names and we would come running up to her wide-open arms for a huge hug and a kiss. She had this demeanor about her which made you feel safe and whole. She worshipped her sister-in-law. Her visits to our home were during her day offs from the White suburbs where she worked as a domestic helper. Aunt Agnes had a peach, smooth complexion. During her weekly visit, she would pull out a loud rouge lipstick and meticulously apply it on our cheeks and lips. Proudly walking us to the mirror, she would stand there watching and grinning, marveling at her brother's daughters. Once the 'show' was over, we would secretly wipe off the rouge and dodge her throughout the evening. As I grew older, I wondered if she was able to discern that her brother's children were of a darker complexion compared to hers. Perhaps it did not matter to her. These were her gifts to us. She groomed our feminine aspects without us even knowing at the time. When we began developing acne, she brought us all kinds of facial ointments and facial soaps. No major family event took place without her. She was a force to be reckoned with but acted with dignity and respect. She knew the traditional customs for observing major events such as burials, weddings, dowry procedures and how to recognize our ancestors.

Zebulon was my father's middle brother. Standing at five foot five my uncle had a take-charge type of a personality, smart, eloquent and confident. He held a highly visible position at Edendale hospital as the head clerk of the hospital. In those days, a Black person in such a position was a huge thing. Every Christmas eve he and his wife would drop off a leg of lamb for us so we dubbed him Father Christmas. Because of his demanding job, a large family and the distance between his home and our home he visited only when he was able to but certainly when there was a crisis. I will always be indebted to him for using his power and influence to get me my first full-time job as a social worker. Because this job was in his town I moved in with his family for three months. My only regret is not having an opportunity to meet and know their youngest brother Uncle Benjamin, until fifty years after my father's death.

Both sides of my parents' families played a vital role in my upbringing. They nurtured me, cultivated my curiosity about the world, allowed me to understand and appreciate family relationships and their significance in enhancing the fiber of a family. They enlightened me about my position within the family but also within society's social and economic stratification. From a child's perspective, my maternal grandmother Lily, and aunts and uncles on both sides, further shaped and influenced my appreciation of being a member of both tribes; Zulu and Xhosa. Through regular traditional practices that symbolized major milestones within the extended families, I began to understand and appreciate each side of my family's traditional customs and/or lack thereof.

Whereas my father migrated from Kwa Xolo, Natal to Johannesburg at seventeen years of age and my mother was born and raised in Pimville, Johannesburg, during my childhood Zulu customs were quite evident compared to Xhosa customs. The only event indicative of Xhosa customs that I can recall was when my brother had to leave home for a two week stay in the mountains in observation of a circumcision ceremony.

Overall, African families in urban areas such as Soweto thrived amidst an external socio-political and economic system that was intensifying its efforts to divide, isolate and deprive them of basic rights to live as human beings and to exercise their God given rights. Yet through this destructive system there evolved a majority of positive, self-sufficient Black families who equipped themselves with strong values to prepare younger generations to explore better choices for themselves.

IV

BOARDING SCHOOL LIFE

Shy, polite and an introvert as a child, I did everything to please my elders, perhaps for attention and approval. As a middle child, very early in my life, I knew I was not of the abject world. My childhood world was one of fantasies. From the subtle memories of the western world shared by my father to the fascinating stories related by my mother about Black South Africans living abroad and exchanges with a pen pal I had from Scotland, I knew I wanted to explore the world. However, first, I had to work hard, earn an education and fulfil my parents' wishes. As a child, I was constantly under my maternal grandmother's wings helping with household chores, running errands, learning how to cook, sew, bake and can fruits. After she passed away, I was a ready and a willing student to anyone willing to teach me something new. A neighbor taught me how to sew. Another neighbor taught me how to make ice-cream while an uncle painstakingly tried to teach me how to play the piano by ear. However, to-date I have not been able to take piano lessons. Though I loved school, I was not a top student. Constantly, I found myself unfairly compared to my older sister who always scored in the top five percent of her class for each marking period, while I was tethered at the tail end. When school reports came out, I would drag myself home hiding my report card while my sister would race home with her report card to brag. Naturally gifted, my sister loved reading. She would wake up in the morning, grab a paper, a book whatever she could lay her hands on, and start reading. For me completing household chores came first, then reading or playing. Nevertheless, I did my best to keep up. Besides, getting an education was not a choice but a must. This was a message we heard from our parents and relatives. In fact, in those days, children were told the only wealth an African parent can bestow to their children was an education. I fully embraced that message but I also knew I had to work hard if I wanted an education so I could become somebody one day. In those days, parents wanted their children to be doctors, lawyers, teachers, nurses or social workers. I often tell a joke about Mother who was in the habit of reminding my older sister and our only brother that she was going to be a doctor and he was going to be a lawyer. When it came to me, she would silently contemplate, 'Hmm! Joey, what are you going to be' and I would respond, 'I don't know?' Every time, my response would be the same. However, I think subconsciously, I pushed myself to prove her wrong.

My move from South Africa's public schools to enrolling at St. Joseph's, a co-educational Catholic boarding school outside Manzini, Swaziland was spearheaded by Uncle George and precipitated in by the introduction of the Bantu Education system of 1953. This law was designed to not only entrench racial separation but served as a landmark for a third-class system of education that prepared and confined Blacks to menial jobs to support the country's mining, manufacturing and service industry. As a result, Black parents began to explore better educational opportunities outside South Africa's borders. Swaziland, Botswana and Lesotho became popular destinations for parents and their children. In order to travel across South

Africa's borders with neighboring countries, one had to have a traveling document. I was ten years old at the time, and could not travel by myself given the distance of two hundred and fifty miles between Johannesburg and Manzini over the un-modernized roads. The ingenuity of our parents to make things happen still amazes me because parents who were eager to have their children out of South Africa's Bantu Education system organized carpools with friends or relatives for transportation. Others with relatives residing in the three protectorates like Swaziland, moved their children to live with relatives. The Nkosi family were family friends who offered to give me a ride to Swaziland since they were also taking their daughter, Fikile, to the same school. So naturally, my mother felt comfortable arranging with them to transport me back and forth to school. Enroute to Swaziland we would make a stop in Witbank, an old coal town which is an hour away from Johannesburg. Here, we picked up Hilda and her younger sister, Veronica, who were also going to St. Joseph's. In subsequent trips, we would always make a stop at their home in Witbank to stretch and have a snack before loading or off-loading on our return trips for the holidays.

Hilda appeared older and mature. Perhaps it was because of her physique and height compared to mine, Fikile, Mr. Nkosi's daughter or Veronica. Hilda was exuberant, chatty, with a beaming smile. Both sisters were good singers. They kept us entertained with songs, jokes, laughter until we fell asleep to be woken up once we reached the Oshoek border post which separated the two countries, South Africa and Swaziland. In another hour and thirty minutes we would reach our destination.

St. Joseph's was located eight miles from the city of Manzini. It was tucked away in a wooded area, approximately five miles from the main highway that carried tourists going to Lorenzo Marques, Mozambique. St. Joseph's was referred to as a mission station because it represented a religious Catholic community of nuns and brothers who were offering educational opportunities to students in a boarding school setting. The campus was spread out in a quadrangle setting with classrooms to the north and east of the quad, the church, priest, brothers' and male students' dormitories were to the west and the kitchen, Nuns' convent and girls' dormitories were to the south of the quad. The majority of students came from different parts of South Africa namely Springs, Germiston, Benoni, Pretoria, Soweto, Witbank and a few students were local from different parts of Swaziland. The synergy from the melting of our diverse social, economic and cultural backgrounds was a source of great inspiration. Because we were all at different levels of growth and maturity with older and younger girls, we learned from each other outside the regular classrooms. There were girls who knew how to sing, write, saw, knit, draw, calculate mathematics, speak different dialects, run and iron helping those who had interests. Swazi girls were raised in the country-side and had better life skills compared to those of us who came from the cities. Swazi girls would often watch us try to collect water from the river or fire wood and break out laughing. However, they would always come to our rescue by teaching us basic life skills of living in the country side. In those five years at St. Joseph's, I learned how to pick our weekly fire wood for the campus' usage, as part of the girls' regular chores. I learned how to collect water in a bucket from the river and carry it on my head like my counterparts, though much to Mother's admonishment of the practice. It was always Swazi girls who came to our rescue when we encountered a snake. Thinking back to those days, it was pitiful to watch how limited and shallow we were because of an upbringing in an urban environment. In spite of our different backgrounds, the spirit of sisterhood was the most powerful glue that bonded us together. Our deficiencies never divided us but offered us with opportunities to learn from each other. Because of the general curiosity about life in the city of Johannesburg and in Soweto, city girls would entertain Swazi girls with true and sometimes made-up stories about life in Soweto. Needless to say, their reactions would be very repulsive with questions and comments like, "How can you live in a place like that?"; "I would never go there." We watched out for each other during study hour by passing on a rolled-up paper in a chain as a warning in case one of us was unaware that the head sister was close by. Another signal used was a cough to warn whoever is still chit-chatting after the night lights have been turned off. This was used whenever a figure in a white habit is spotted, stealthy walking along the rows of beds to make sure everyone was accounted for. Once Mother superior gives us her blessings, and the glass doors were shut, silence would prevail as we all gently fell into a slumber for the night.

Campus life was strictly regimented and monotonous. The day began with an early rise at five a.m. to complete varied chores, followed by a shower, a non-descriptive breakfast, then lining up for a check of our uniform by Sister Sebastian or whoever was in charge for that week to make sure we were appropriately groomed, shoes-shined, and with clean socks before entering the church for daily prayers. This was a routine for both morning and evening prayers. The morning schedule was followed by church prayers whereby we would line up again for school assembly, then march to our respective classrooms. There would be an hours break for lunch before a return to class. School would finally break at four p.m. We would have a free time of two hours until supper. Supper was immediately followed by a study period of one hour followed by preparations for bed time. By the time we went to bed, we were exhausted. Chit-chats were limited before the dormitory lights were turned off. In addition to having a structure in my life, I learned self-discipline, hard work, sharing and respecting others. I got to know that my guardian angel was constantly besides me protecting and guiding me. I took these teaching in literal terms. Anything I wanted, I prayed to God. I prayed for my father's soul and those of all the relatives who had left us to rest in peace. I prayed to God to grant my mother strength to heal and shoulder the burden of caring for all five of us. In addition to knowing and believing in a higher power, I felt protected.

Everyone can attest to moments of stupidity in their early years. Mine was with a friend. During one of our roll calls, my friend and I thought we could outsmart Sister Sebastian. Frankly it was one of the most absurd things to do because Sister Sebastian was young, tough and wide-eyed. Sometimes when she looked at you with her piercing blue eyes, one felt immediately defeated. That week, my friend and I had run out of laundry soap. So, because we could not do our laundry, our uniform and socks for the week were not washed. Despite the nasty odor from day's sweat, we had convinced ourselves no one would notice. However, as we were getting ready to line up, girls who were walking behind us started giggling with silly remarks about what they described as visibly dirty socks. I guess my friend was annoyed listening to their silly cracks. She quickly motioned me to join her as we left the line and started running toward the bathroom as if there was an emergency. Once we got into the bathroom area, she quickly rolled out toilet paper and meticulously rolled it around the ankles of my feet, easily folding it inside the shoes to look like socks. In return, I had to do likewise and get the toilet paper fitted in the same style to make it look like white socks. We then hurriedly left the bathroom to join the line walking past Sister Sebastian. Since I was ahead of my friend, I was not stopped. As my friend followed behind me, I could only hear Sister's deep voice calling out, "Hazel, come back here. What do you have there?" Unbeknownst to me, Hazel's toilet paper cover had slightly rolled out of her left ankle, to the back of her shoe, and everyone behind her was laughing because as she walked, she was stepping on it. The resounding laughter caught Sister's attention. As Sister Sebastian who could speak in Swati yelled out to Hazel and me rushing over to literally grab each of our hands and removing us from the line. In a stern voice, she ordered us to wait until everyone had entered the church. We entered the church with her and were ordered to sit in the last row where she could see us. The following morning, we had to report to the laundry room for our punishment. The irony is that we could not do our laundry because our punishment only required us to do the laundry from the convent. However, we both learned a lesson in that we made it a practice to have our laundry done every weekend when it was laundry time.

My belief in the power of prayer was, and still is very profound. I prayed to God to guide me through the pressures of my youth. Like my friends, I wanted to attract the most popular guy at school, yet I was very shy. Then, I thought it was regretful that none of the guys found me attractive. Unlike today, girls did not approach guys and when that did not happen no one lost sleep over it. It did not destroy you. Young girls were raised and socialized to hold their heads high, believing someone was out there for you.

The last year of junior high, I had to apply to another boarding school that went through form four and form five, the equivalence of grade eleven and grade twelve in the United States. Luckily, I got accepted at a national boarding school which was more liberal compared to the strict regimented Catholic boarding school I was in. Indeed, the following year I started my eleventh grade. I got to meet my teachers. My teachers were an interesting group with different backgrounds. There were those who were local natives, one had studied abroad and brought home his European spouse as was typical of many who studied abroad. Four members of the teaching staff were originally from South Africa but were then living in Swaziland. Two White teachers came from the United States. They were part of the peace-Corp who had been assigned to different parts of Africa with the exception of South Africa. This group of teachers were highly educated. They had high standards and expectations when it came to academic performances. As much as it was somewhat of a liberal school in comparison to my previous school, the message was quite clear, students were to be treated as mature individuals. They were to be respected and allowed to exercise their rights but with responsibility. Obviously for someone coming out of a restrictive boarding school setting as I was, this was going to be paradise, but not exactly.

It is here where temptations got in the way. I befriended a feisty, mischievous girl named Lea. Given my shy nature, I became more of a follower to Lea's mischiefs. Our first violation of the school's policy on conduct occurred when we missed a roll call following a school trip for the school's athletic teams to participate at a regional athletic competition. Lea had arranged with her second cousin to pick us up from the sporting arena to go to her cousin's apartment for lunch. We left the sporting arena without permission. We brought a change of clothing to wear so we could disguise ourselves and take off our identifiable school uniform. Once at Lea's cousin's apartment, we felt no one could see nor know where we came from. After sitting down for lunch, Lea's sister who was accompanying us took over and served us table-wine with lunch. Both of us had never had table wine before, so naturally we got sick. We became afraid to return back to the games for fear it would be obvious we were tipsy and sick. So, we prolonged our stay. When the day got darker, we panicked. Since the apartment was in a high-rise building, we had to take the elevator downstairs. Talk about bad luck! As we waited for the elevator to take us downstairs, the doors opened, we walked in. From the crowd that was packed inside the elevator, one familiar voice sarcastically asked, "Where were you girls? Who were you visiting? Weren't you supposed to stay with the group?" Lea's cousin took over trying to answer on our behalf but could not go very far because this was Angie's voice, one of the teachers at the school who was undeterred. She recited the school's policy and reminded us we were going to face disciplinary actions when we got back. Lea, myself and her cousin walked out of that elevator in silence and embarrassment. The truth is, we had embarrassed ourselves. By the time we got back to the sporting arena, the buses had been boarded and were waiting for those who were still missing. My friend and I were in that group that was missing. Needless to say, the teachers who thought something terrible had happened to us, were furious when they saw us. The ride back to our campus was long, uncomfortable with cruel snipes and jokes from school mates. Since Lea and I were not the only ones who had violated the school's policy, we kind of assumed the violation of campus behavior was going to be minimal. On a Monday of the following week, we reported to the administration office as advised and were brought in front of the school's disciplinary committee. Again, the consolation was that we were not the only ones. There were ten of us facing various infractions. The committee spared my friend and I from school suspension or dismissal. It recommended two days of out of school punishment. I was very shaken, embarrassed and disappointed in myself. This was one of the first situations that made me realize I could not afford getting myself in these types of bad situations. I had to be careful in my involvement with Lea.

After weathering this storm, another one was about to happen. This one involved boyfriend/girlfriend type relationships which were foreign to me. Much as I was flattered by classmates who made passes, I was equally afraid of being with a boy. Being a product of Catholic/Anglican upbringing with five years of Catholic boarding school experience, I did not know what was expected. So, Lea took it upon herself to be the conduit for any boy who showed an interest in me. One of these boys was the son of the owner of a local Portuguese Café in town which, basically, was one of the main eating places in town. This was where, each time the college brought us into town for a field trip, we would order take-outs or have sit-in meals. Tony was handsome and somewhat shy. He was limited in English but fluent in Portuguese. He had a crush on me. At the time, I was not aware until my friend told me she had noticed that each time I walked into the store with her, Tony's face lit up. I dismissed her view as wishful thinking but began to notice as Tony would try to hold my hand or want to accompany us when we left the café which was odd. Lea liked the idea that we got whatever we wanted from the store, without paying a penny because Tony would not charge us anything. I found it embarrassing. However, Lea saw nothing wrong with it. Whenever the trip took us to town, I would beg Lea not to go to the Portuguese Café but she would reason with me, "We get ample food without paying, so what's the big deal?" However, she refused to see my point of view that taking Tony's gifts implied I had an interest too. Ordinarily, we would order take outs but in one of our trips to the store, Tony had reserved a table for us in the Café, a booth. He invited us in. I was in panic for several reasons. This town was very small. Everybody knew everybody. Both my paternal uncle George and aunt, his wife were well known in this town. In fact, the Café used to be my aunt's hang-out after my uncle's death. She met with friends at this café. Several times she had brought me to this café. What if she showed up while I was dining at a table with the owner's son? Besides, much as in this British Protectorate there was an openness to interracial dating, I was not so sure what my aunt's views were on interracial relationships. I shared all these fears with Lea who quickly dismissed me as ridiculous.

After taking our favorite order, chicken peri-peri, Toni joined us, sat next to me and held my hand. I was uneasy, sweating and just could not look at him. Meanwhile Lea who was sitting across from us was giving me an eye of admonition. I tried to relax and respond to Toni's touch but the entire time I was feeling awkward. I broke loose from his hand and stood up in protest. Toni realized I was uncomfortable and tried to avoid making a scene. He agreed to leave us to enjoy the meal and returned a short while later. This time he asked a pointed question: "Did I like him?"

Lea responded, "Of course, look at her smile." Toni's face lit up. He asked if we wanted anything from the front store. Lea ran her list. At this point, it became pretty obvious Lea was using me. I got up to leave but Toni who obviously did not understand the dynamics at play, insisted that I sit and relax while he went to get the grocery. By this time, I was disgusted with Lea and we began exchanging unkind words to each other in our language. When Toni returned, Lea thanked him and he reached out to plant a kiss on my lips, I immediately looked the other way. The days of free groceries would end that day. I made it clear to Lea I was not going to be used. That visit signaled my last trip with Lea to the Portuguese Café. As luck would have it, three years thereafter, my aunt took me to the Portuguese Cafe where she was meeting a friend for lunch. Surprisingly, Toni was not there. Part of me was disappointed. Perhaps I wanted to see if the spark was still there three years thereafter or if he would recognize me. I am still not sure why I was so disappointed not to see him. Fast forward to five years later, I learned from a friend that Toni was dating a popular socialite in town. Amongst many experiences of my youth where drastic disasters could have happened to ruin my future, I often reflect on that experience with Toni and wonder what would have become of me if my guardian angel had abandoned me and I had allowed temptation and Lea's selfish desires to prevail. Going separate ways with Lea was God sent.

My final year of high school proved disastrous. Though I had not firmed up my plans as to what college, I wanted to go to following high school, I fully understood that my opportunities were limited in entering the University of Lesotho, Botswana and Swaziland because I had performed poorly in the Cambridge high school level exams. As a result, I had to repeat English Literature before graduating high school. Needless to say, my world was crushed. I had to stay back while a few friends of mine went to the university in Botswana. Others were recruited by Swaziland's Standard Bank. The latter, was not open to graduates who were citizens of South Africa. I stayed in Swaziland with my uncle's wife and her children. With the help of a tutor from William Pitcher College where she taught, I successfully finished the year to graduate from high school. During the course of that year, I had applied to the University of Zululand in South Africa and was accepted. I dreaded going back to South Africa but I had no other choice but to return back to my country.

V

THE WONDERS OF COLLEGE LIFE

Returning to South Africa for college education, the journey proved to be quite fascinating in terms of broadening my perspective about higher education and the culture surrounding it, plus the influences of America's hippy movement in South Africa's universities. The university I attended was one of the ethnic designated Bantu universities of South Africa. Named after the Zulu tribe, the University of Zululand was located in the province of Natal. It is one of the Black universities which were structured in accordance with the regional Bantu Homeland policies of equal but separate development, a policy which appeared to be patterned after the reservations policies of North America. In those days, going to college was a big deal because it elevated one's social stature. I desperately wanted to attend college like my counterparts who went to the University of Lesotho, Botswana and Swaziland.

My thoughts of mingling with college mates who spoke big words and bragged about abstract lectures on constitutional law or child psychology, were quite daunting. I was eager to learn and take the challenge of performing at that level of education. I imagined myself at some point bragging about a specific subject area in my field as well. Since I was already accustomed to waking up at five from my boarding school experience, it became easy to get into the practice of waking up to study. While lectures were in English, some of the Afrikaans speaking professors' pronunciations were hard to decipher. This was indeed a different educational environment. Whereas in boarding school, our teachers looked us in the eyes to make sure we were listening attentively and absorbing the information, it was completely different there. The professors I had in college walked into a classroom with no paper or book with notes, and began lecturing, jotting a word or two on the blackboard. It was fascinating to watch. The content was so abstract that it was safe to say they had memorized their lectures. During a lecture, there was no direct eye contact with students, no discussions nor questions needing further elaboration. Instead, our professors had their gaze to the back of the classroom, above our heads. They offered little if any explanations nor presented hypothetical scenarios about what they were describing. For the majority of us whose mother tongue was not English, it became very helpful to either read one's textbooks before or after a lecture. Personally, I admired their style. It suggested to me this was what you do when you are highly educated. You do not attempt to explain but you leave it to the student to figure it out. Odd as it looked, this was the culture; far different from what I have come to know about pedagogical principles to teaching and learning. I enjoyed learning, and did not mind doing double duty for my learning. When I started in my career, I knew I did not want to be that type of a professor who memorizes and fails to help students connect with a concept through examples. Despite their classroom performance, these professors were accessible for individual conferences after each lecture and for group consultations. One thing about my college experience, it subtly introduced me to think in a socially stratified manner, it was them and us.

In college there were all kinds of students from serious learners, trend-setters, party animals, show-boaters, thugs, marriage-seekers to the misplaced ones. Whenever I watch legal shows on TV with lawyers offering their legal expert opinions, I think of a college mate who was a show-boater. Each Friday during the library's closing hours, he would stall the checkout line with thick volumes of law encyclopedias and law books while surveying and making jokes about what others were checking out. With his thick and short stature, he would finally exit the library, walk down the stairs with books tucked under each of his arms, tilted to a side from heaviness. While descending from the library steps, he liked to glance around to survey who might be close by to listen to some article of the law he was reading. On one occasion, my roommate and I happened to exit the library about the same time as he was checking out his books for the weekend. He exited the library right behind us then started describing a paper he was writing and how he needed to frame his arguments within the context of a case that was argued years ago. It felt awkward. We had no clue as to what he was talking about. This was out of our league. Undoubtedly brilliant, he was one of the best braggards on campus. It was fascinating to listen to him debate his peers, quoting significant rulings that became landmark rulings in South Africa. By all standards, his intelligence, passion for debates on law, stature, aggressive style and voice command, had geared him up for a successful law career.

College life was fun and demanding. I discovered that a college education was a multifaceted experience designed to prepare one to serve as a member of a civil society by making significant contributions through knowledge and participation in social, cultural and political activities, it was a good place to be trained for the world of work. I had an eye for fashion and I was attracted to medicine. The latter was much of an unrealistic dream given my weaknesses in math and the sciences. I admired fashion-conscientious female professors. Perhaps I got my love of fashion from my mother who modeled femininity, etiquette and dressing like a 'lady' as she would say. College taught me varied styles of dressing which were inspired by American trends and culture from casual bell-bottoms, mini-skirts, dashiki dresses to formal cocktail attires. This also involved how to conduct oneself in social circles. One of the things we learned from older girls was the importance of drawing a distinction between us as college students from those young girls we left back home. Self-regulation around alcohol consumption took center stage each time we socialized with older girls who were our seniors at college. Beer drinking was looked down upon and perceived to be un-lady-like. Drinking champagne at parties was considered much more acceptable notwithstanding the morning after's throbbing headache. I do not think we knew then that champagne was rated based on quality, brand or price. Obviously as college kids we drank what we could afford. All that was important was when you got to a party and you were asked, 'what will you drink?' You always had to stand out from the rest by mentioning; 'oh, I'll take a glass of champagne'. Anything associated with sophistication was the name of the game. It also meant one had to be at their best for the annual Spring ball dance concerts which were organized by our student government. The women had to honor the dress code of long evening gowns and their accessories. Likewise, men had to wear clean shirts, a tie and no sneakers. Our men counterparts were truly gentlemen. The way they would conduct themselves was so much reflective of college educated men. Moreover, many had girlfriends on campus. So, it was important to make the best impression. Unfortunately, a handful of our men would visit taverns in the neighboring town prior to our big event and create unwelcome scenes when they showed up on campus inebriated, sweating, wearing dirty and smelly sneakers. The stifling odor from alcohol would be so unbearable that the senior members of the student government would ask them to leave only to be met with protests. Though college policies and admission policies to the hall hosting the event were known to everyone, namely a clean shirt, tie and dress shoes, they would crash the event and create a scene.

As soon as they made their entrance, the mood would change as jeers and boos reverberated throughout the hall. The rowdiness, fighting and cursing of members of the band hired to entertain us was one of the low points of our annual Spring Ball. Sadly, sometimes it would be difficult to discern if these men were part of our student body or from the local community. Every year, this is what we had to contend with. Ladies would sit tight folding their arms as a signal that they were not interested in being asked to dance by any of the unruly characters. As the night progressed, so did the unruly mob with their sweat dripping faces on the dance floor. The strong odor from filthy sneakers and the smell of old beer permeating through the hall and nauseating could not be tolerated by many. The enjoyment of the evening would gradually dissipate as the drunkards fell asleep in their chairs and slowly the fashionably-dressed ladies would leave the hall escorted by the good guys to their dormitories. This was always the downside to the otherwise fun-filled campus events.

Financially, it was difficult to stay in college. Mother and I were determined to pull through, knowing that the family's finances could not possibly allow me to cover tuition, housing costs, transportation, books and fees. One of the most unforgettable days was when I received a letter from the registrar's office threatening me with dismissal if the owed tuition was not paid by the due date. It so happened that another friend who actually was a neighbor back home, had received the same warning. We both arranged to go to a nearby post office to send our mothers telegrams. As we walked from our dormitory to the post office, we met two White middle-aged women, one a nun. They seemed to be admiring the campus. One of the women appeared to have a physical disability. She was limping. As we approached them, they stopped and we exchanged greetings. They began engaging us in a conversation about the campus. We immediately tried to limit the conversation, and explained to them that we were rushing to the post office before it closed. They offered to wait for us, since the post office was not too far away from where we were standing.

On our way back, they were still waiting. As we started walking, heading toward the campus, they asked us to take them on a campus tour. We agreed. They were curious to know about our family backgrounds the areas we were pursuing in our education, our religion and the parish we were affiliated with back home, and why we owed money. Some of the questions were quite invasive. As we were both practicing Catholics then, we shared everything. The lady who was limping, Ms. Powers had a special interest in my story. She took down information about our parish priest since we both worshipped at St. Martins. Our tour ended. They took photos, we accompanied them back to their car then headed back to our dormitories. Two weeks later, I received a letter from my priest informing me that he had received a request from a Ms. Powers to visit my home and report back to her with information about my family background which I surmised was a home study. The outcome of that home study was a full payment of my tuition, housing, book allowance and fees for that entire year to include what I owed the university. A caveat to that offer was for me as a recipient not to contact her.

Ms. Powers' gesture taught me two profound things. Not to paint every White South African as heartless but to be reminded that there were many Helen Suzmans out there. Ms. Powers did not know me from a bar of soap nor was she obligated to do anything about my situation however, out of the kindness of her heart, she offered help to set me on the path to success. Secondly, I got to understand the value of giving back, of improving others' circumstances to make them better without fanfare. If everyone were to be a Ms. Powers, the world would have less sufferings and children would not be going to bed without food. In order to stay in college for the following year, Mother encouraged me to apply for a bursary from the South African Legion because my father had served during World War II. Indeed, I applied and was granted a bursary that carried me through graduation with a condition that I serve the City Council of Johannesburg for two years upon the completion of my studies.

It was during winter and summer breaks from college that I took notice at how I had drifted away from my friends in Soweto. Actually, this drift began when I was in my senior year in Swaziland. Each time word got around that I was back, my local friends would come by for a social visit. The first few visits were fine. My friends' main curiosity was about the general experience of being away from home in a boarding school. Life in a boarding school was often associated with prison-like living conditions and treatment. However, I often shared the positive aspects of a boarding school which they found enlightening. By the time I entered college, I was curious about learning. I wanted to associate with people who were much smarter than I was, who read a lot, spoke eloquently and had higher career goals. I felt I could be inspired by others who were much more gifted in order to be a better person, and to make better decisions about my future. To my mother's credit, she is the one who often reminded me, 'you have nothing in common with them. What are you gaining from these friendships?' She was right. However, it took me a while to understand and accept what she meant. Mother was a classist and at times her attitude bothered me. From my perspective, it felt like I was abandoning old friends and somehow viewed myself as better. As I became more aware of our value differences, I stopped my association with them but remained friendly.

My college roommate and I were strangers at the beginning but with time, became best friends. We had the same passion and determination about learning. We were selective in terms of which social events to attend/not to attend because our priority was about our academic progress. I introduced my roommate to my study habits from boarding school of waking up at four to study until six a.m. It paid off. I would describe the lifestyle pattern that we developed for ourselves as moderately disciplined. We had a clear grasp of where we came from since we both had our mothers as the bread-winners at home, we knew we could not afford to play around but had to focus on our education. At the beginning, neither one of us dated on campus but she later did find a boyfriend on campus. I chose to hold on to my boyfriend who was back home. We became selective when it came to campus entertainment in terms of which event to attend, and whose parties to attend. There were parties thrown by male students in their resident halls, we shied away from those because of the scandalous aftermaths of most of them. One of the most disgusting things they would do was to 'set-up' certain women so they would embarrass themselves after having fun with dancing and consuming alcohol then expose them thereafter. The exposures were done by posting a sketch of whatever scene they choose, then display it on a commonly visited bulletin board. While the identity of the person would be concealed, the reader could easily decipher the identity of the individual in question, by analyzing the write-up to the post. Whoever wrote those scandalous pieces, was a brilliant person whose own identity remained a top secret up to the time we graduated.

Graduation from college was a huge event for my family but most importantly for Mother. I was the first in the family to graduate from college. She had bought a fancy beige hat to match her hand bag and a cream-colored coat for the graduation ceremony. To my surprise, she had also organized transportation with an uncle to drive us to Natal, Zululand, a three hundred and sixty-one mile drive from Johannesburg. Uncle Maphumulo owned a Mercedes Benz which, by the way he took care of it, it was very dear to his heart. It was a well-maintained car. As long as I had known my uncle, no one ever rode in that car except when there was a funeral. Hence, I was surprised at his generosity to drive three hundred and sixty-one miles from Johannesburg to Natal for my graduation. Indeed, I felt very special. My roommate's home was at Umlazi, in Durban. She had offered to host my family on their arrival for the graduation ceremony. During and after the graduation ceremony, it was heartwarming to watch my mother in her glory, so gratified to see the daughter she often asked, 'what are you going to be?' finally make her so proud. Watching her in that crowd during graduation ceremonies, beaming with joy, made me feel satisfied for making her to finally witness the fruits of her labor.

The fun of college life, the freedom of doing whatever you want, whenever you want, had ended. Young adulthood was now looking in my eyes. My next step was supposed to be finding a job, which I did. My paternal uncle had organized a job for me which meant I had to go and live with his family and return home on weekends. This was definitely not a good arrangement. The good thing was that I could now work and make a financial contribution. However, within two months of that job, the City Council of Johannesburg offered me a job as a social worker. It felt good to be back home. The next societal expectation was for me to get married and have children. Unfortunately, I had broken my relationship with a high school sweetheart soon after my graduation from college.

Maurice was the love of my life. We met during one of our train trips from Johannesburg to boarding school in Swaziland. Mother had accompanied me to the Johannesburg Park Station to board my train to Swaziland. By coincidence, Maurice's mother was also there. It turned out that the two knew each other. As registered nurses employed by the Johannesburg Health Department serving in the Soweto health clinics, they had worked together. She was also accompanying her son who attended St. Christophers in Mbabane, a boy's school where my brother also went to school. I do not recall how the two of us were introduced. However, we started talking. He was talkative, laid back, somewhat awkward, a charmer with a high sense of humor. We did not get a chance to know each other until the following morning when we transferred from the train to a bus which took us past the Oshoek border post with Swaziland, to our respective destinations. Maurice did most of the talking telling me about his family, his sister, a cousin, his responsibilities to his family. I was quite impressed by the level of responsibility he had toward his family. I can remember so well how dazed I was after he planted a kiss on my lips when we parted. I figured, that was what I had to feel when I was attracted to a member of the opposite sex. From that point on, we started corresponding frequently through letters. During winter and summer breaks, we visited each other. He became my steady boyfriend. We cared deeply for each other. During holidays, I always looked forward to spending time with him. Ours was a pure, innocent love affair of holding hands, kissing, listening to his favorite music by Stevie Wonder. I was a special woman to him. He demonstrated it in so many ways. While in college, I would receive a collection of expensive cosmetic gifts for birthdays or as Christmas gifts sent by mail. He was never a lavish spender and that made every gift I got from him so special. One of the most memorable gifts he gave me was my very first opportunity to fly in an airplane.

Percy Sledge, a popular American R&B singer of the early 1970s visited Soweto for the first time in 1970. This was while I was in college in Zululand. I was so thrilled to get a letter from Maurice with an air-ticket to come home because he had bought tickets for us to go to the show. Did I mention, this was my very first time flying? It was a big deal. My college friends could not believe it, 'You mean you are flying overnight to a Percy Sledge show? Lucky you. I wish I had a boyfriend who would do that for me'.

Little did I know that our five-year romantic relationship was soon to fall apart at the seams, through no fault of his but mine. After my graduation which Maurice had attended, I broke up with him. I was guilty, remorseful and wanted a way to make amends with him. I approached a common friend of ours that I respected. She and her husband were older but were our strong supporters whom we looked up to. I wanted her guidance on how to navigate the situation I was in with Maurice. I will never forget her demeanor on that particularly day. The regular warm embraces, kisses on both cheeks, tea with biscuits or scones, were not forthcoming. Rather, I was met with a stern and cold look. It was uncomfortable. She sat me down, not to admonish me for what I had done but to express the devastation that Maurice had suffered. I will never forget her description of what I meant to Maurice. She asserted, "Do you realize you were like a diamond in the palm of his hand?" My eyes welling with tears, I tried to explain myself. She cut through my sentence, stating, "It is too late now. The damage has been done. I know he does not want to ever see you again." Well, that was it for me. I pulled myself together, thanked her and left. Because of the proximity of his business to where our friends lived I knew he was watching me as I disappeared from his orbit. My world was shattered.

As life would have it, years thereafter we had another chance encounter. I visited him at his business location with a common friend of ours. Maurice was visibly surprised to see me. We hugged, made light jokes and conversations about nothing. He seemed quite happy but something had changed. His hysteric laughter was new to me. I wondered if he was drinking a lot or just stressed because of the business he was running for his dad. As he would normally do, he pulled up a Stevie Wonder record titled, *Joy Inside My Tears* and started playing it over and over again, insisting I should listen to the lyrics. It was obvious we could not rekindle what we once had. He was a broken man and I was responsible for it. A year thereafter, I heard it through the grape vine that he was getting married. Needless to say, my hope that one day we could be together again was completely dashed. I had to lick my wounds and face my world alone. The possibilities of getting married had moved farther away from me. To this day, when I play that Stevie Wonder song, I listen to the lyrics and wonder who was that special woman who brought him joy inside those tears. I will never know. Maurice died in the early 1980s. By that time, I had already left South Africa for America. It was my brother who called to inform me about his passing. They knew each other because they were school mates at St. Christopher's boarding school. My brother might have explained what led to his death but I have a mental block. I cannot remember because I was too shaken to learn about his passing at such a young age. He was and still is, very dear to my heart. I still play that song every so often.

Perhaps out of pity, friends of mine decided to be match makers. They introduced me to someone who had graduated from our university three years prior to my graduating year. He was older and much too serious about life. The first time I met him, I was not particularly interested. He was too mature. His conversations were boring. He liked to engage in intellectual discussions about the country's economy, a subject that was frankly of little interest and far beyond my level of comprehension. I was a social worker with interest in supporting regular people as they solved their problems. I wasn't interested in understanding the economic disparities between White and Black communities. Only in my adulthood did I realize how much I would have gained if only I had listened. Nevertheless, at that time in my life, I was more interested in having fun like going to the disco to dance, having romantic picnics, taking short and long distant trips with scenic views to uplift my spirits. His ideas of outings were to attend lecture series on economics at a local university. I found these lectures too abstract, boring and way above my head. Though he would try to simplify the content, I just hated them. Unfortunately for me, Mother was quite impressed by this fellow. She thought he was polished, a gentleman from a good family. The fact that he was preparing to open his own business, added another star on Mother's list of stars. As is the customary practice in our culture for marriage proposals, he planned to send his family representatives to meet with my family for my hand in marriage. This process was also followed by agreements on dowry payments from his side to my family. Granted, my generation despised dowry but it was something one could not protest. When that happened I realized I was done. No one was interested in how I felt. Everything moved hastily according to what my elders wanted. Both his family and mine met for ritual observations and the completion of dowry payments which is a customary practice. Wedding arrangements followed. I was married in church in a beautiful ceremony surrounded by family and friends. Whereas a bride is supposed to be sparkling from inside out, I was empty inside. Years later when I had a chance to review photos that were taken during the wedding ceremony, particularly the one that was taken when we exchanged our vows, I was filled with sadness and broke down crying. I was not only angry at myself but at him as well. He knew I did not love him. I was never kind, warm but impatient, and rude toward him. He became abusive, stalking me everywhere I went. Co-workers became aware of my fear to leave the office, where I worked, alone. Needless to say, I never kept a copy of any of those wedding photos. It is part of my life that I never want to revisit nor to acknowledge to myself that it existed. It should have never happened. However, when you are young and obliged to the elders in the family, knowing there is no other outlet, you get trapped in those sad, unhappy marriages. Mine lasted a year. Loyalty to the family has its downfalls. I see it and hear about it so often. Moreover, I have been a victim of it as well. To some, it might sound ridiculous to hear me use the term, victim. Though I was twenty-five years of age, I was still obligated to follow my elders' advice and recommendations. Deep down I knew they wanted the best for me in terms of someone who would take care of me materially. However, they missed the part of physical and mental attraction which was missing for me. This was a sad chapter of my life.

I returned home to my parents' house the following year. To my surprise, friends from college who would come to visit me at my parents' home would try to convince me to go back because as they would put it, "all marriages have problems." I would ask myself, "What part were they missing?" I was in a fixed and abusive marriage. The marriage was for his convenience and not for my happiness. In all fairness, Mother took it in her stride. She understood the emotional tumult of confusion, disappointment and hurt that I was going through. Two years later, she sat me down to tell me about what she described as a bad omen. She related that during those three months after the wedding, she spotted a train of ants coming out of the preserved wedding cake. Customarily, a piece of a wedding cake is saved until the birth of the married couple's first child. I did not know what to think or feel about that revelation. All I knew was that I needed to recover from that experience and look on the brighter side of life again. I was only twenty-five years old and definitely did not deserve the misery of sacrificing my life by staying in an empty marriage to save face.

VI

STUDENTS' UPRISING OF 1976

I had heard stories about the Sharpeville massacre of 1960 where police killed close to three hundred children and adults following a peaceful protest against the forced removal of families.

I had shelved this incidence about the country's past as if it would never return. However, I was wrong. By the mid-1970s, the disenchantment over South Africa's Bantu Education seemed to be boiling over due to an escalation of tensions between high school students and the Ministry of Bantu Education's persistence to use Afrikaans as a medium of instruction. This generation of students was beginning to analyze the value of their education long-term and beyond South Africa. Their bone of contention was that Afrikaans was not a universal language that would prepare them for the global market. They were advocating for the use of English as a medium of instruction so as to prepare them to compete fairly with other nations, in the open labor market. The self-consciousness movement was enlightening to many of us, to look beyond the superficial status of being a rightful Black urban citizen of South Africa to one who is entitled to all the rights bestowed to a White South African.

Piecing together the events of June sixteenth depended on where one was on that day. One thing that is generally known is that it was well orchestrated by high school students throughout

Soweto. They held their main protest demonstrations in a centralized part of Orlando West, near Orlando West high school, the Holy Cross Anglican Church and within walking distances to homes of stronghold members of banned political parties, of Pan National Congress and African National Congress respectfully, in the likes of Mandela, Sisulu, Mothopeng and Bishop Tutu. At the time, I was working for the City Council of Johannesburg to fulfil a bursary obligation following the completion of my studies in social work at the University of Zululand. My office of employment was located in Senoane Municipal offices, approximately five miles away from where the protests were taking place. However, there were similar activities taking place in our area as we were in close proximity to Sekano Ntoane High school, one of Soweto's high schools. On that particular day, my colleagues and I were expecting our supervisor, Dr. Egelstein who ordinarily would drive from his office in the city of Johannesburg to Soweto to conduct supervision. While waiting for him, we were also sharing with each other our concerns over his safety because as a White person, he would be traveling through some of the hot spots of Soweto where protests against Bantu Education had already been reported on radio. In addition, there were road blocks already reported and we wondered how he would navigate his way through these areas to get to where we were in deep Soweto. In fact, members of the White community were warned not to enter Soweto for their safety. To be clear, it was the law of the land for White people not to enter designated Black areas. However, White members of the City Council of Johannesburg who held key positions in the administration of offices throughout Soweto, were granted special provisions of employment in Soweto. As a social worker by profession, Dr. Egelstein was one of the supervisors for Black social workers

81

hired by the City Council of Johannesburg to provide services to residents of Soweto. He was a man of integrity with a passion and commitment to his work. On that fateful day, we had hoped that he would heed the warnings and not come for our regular supervisory meeting, that he would, alternatively, be escorted out to safety by members of the South African police force who by that time were all over Soweto. The events of that day were so unprecedented that many White people who had worked in Soweto, interacted with Black people felt safe and minimized the seriousness of the day, despite speculations and warnings.

One of the greatest challenges I have experienced since that fateful day is to piece together what actually happened to Dr. Egelstein. The only part that resonates with me is that my colleagues and I were in our office building waiting patiently for him, at the same time we were worried about our own safety, getting out of the area and making our way safely to our respective places of residence became excessively scary. The pace of news was slow as landlines were over-worked with busy signals. It was during that time that we got word that all municipal workers were being dismissed for their safety as municipal buildings were being destroyed. Uncertain of his whereabouts and hoping that he would be escorted out of Soweto to safety, we continued waiting in panic. The recollection of what eventually happened to him is too vague to remember. At times I wonder if the sight of the brutal attack traumatized me to the extent that I have blocked it from my memory? I seem to remember him trying to find shelter under a desk table as we were being pelted with stones. At the same time, I cannot place the rest of us anywhere in that office. Did we run out? Were we let go? Was he able to escape? How? None of us was harmed. To this day, I am haunted by the image of him under a desk table. That evening, I got a copy of a local newspaper to see if there was any coverage of what had happened at our office but nothing was reported other than the photo of the youngest victim of police shootings in Orlando West. Dr. Egelstein's commitment to the work we were doing must have been the driving force for him to still honor his appointment to meet us for our weekly case discussions, despite the dangers. To him, we were colleagues not subordinates. During case discussions, he always came through with suggestions, options and solutions of solving the problems of families and individuals, that were partly a product of the apartheid system, in the most humane way. He would always remind us to structure our solutions within the framework of apartheid laws. He was always open to nonconventional solutions particularly to situations that involved the repatriation of the elderly from urban areas to 'the homelands'. Under apartheid laws, elderly Black people in urban areas like Johannesburg were viewed as non-contributors to South Africa's economic growth. Therefore, to ease housing shortages, it was common practice to remove those elderly who were home owners and resettle them in the homelands. In light of the housing shortage, Dr. Egelstein endorsed his social workers' practice of matching newly married couples with elderly home owners to live and basically take care of the elderly owner and in return have a place to stay. Amidst frequent complaints, disenchantment and frustrations over lack of financial support from the City Council for the work we did, Dr. Edelstein brought meaning and value to social workers in Soweto.

During the state of emergency that was declared throughout Soweto following the 1976 riots our work was suspended for approximately two months. The municipal building was not functional. Soweto remained volatile after police had killed several people, resulting in a state of mayhem as people charged at police with stones, burning their homes and government facilities. The main entrance roads to Soweto were blocked using burning tires to prevent military trucks that were dispatched to restore law and order, from passing through. However, those military trucks finally came and occupied every corner of Soweto with military personnel in camouflage uniforms shooting indiscriminately at people. As many people were hit by stray bullets, it was never advisable to be out. Soweto had been transformed overnight into a war zone. A report I read later equated Soweto in those days to Beirut.

When work at the city council municipal offices finally resumed, a centralized venue was selected on the outskirts of Soweto, and closer to the city of Johannesburg where we could all meet. Those meetings were tense as Black social workers were grieving for their innocent loved ones who had been shot by police while members of the White staff sat silently and occasionally recounting where they were when those demonstrations started. The mood gradually got better as all of us started sharing our thoughts and feelings particularly over the loss that we had all suffered. Following the debriefing, we were organized into small groups to begin planning our work. We were allowed to work from home briefly but eventually we were able to return to our offices. Every one of us who worked at the previous office where Dr. Egelstein met his fate that day, was relocated to another office.

VII

DETENTION AND SOLITARY CONFINEMENT

Life in Soweto completely changed for many residents and for the country after June sixteenth 1976. The trust we had amongst neighbors and friends was dissipating as the South African security police began rounding up people who were suspected to have been the instigators of the riots. Friends, neighbors and in some instances family members were being used to spy on each other in exchange for money, lighter sentences if they were involved or exoneration. Maintaining a distance from friends and just being cautious of who you were befriending, made life quite nerve-racking. On a personal level, there were a number of things that were beginning to converge and force me to take a serious look at my life. I was going through a tough time regaining my sense of pride after that failed marriage. At the same time, the experience I had just gone through, with young people being killed for rightfully advocating for their rights to a decent system of education and the brutal killing of a human being who was doing so much good for my people but because of the color of skin had to die in such a senseless way, made me take a second look at the insidious harm of apartheid. The apartheid system was turning kind, and peace-loving people into animals. I was beginning to see the true essence of South Africa that I had systematically avoided dealing with or shielded myself from it by escaping to Swaziland. The social disconnects from college friends who seemed to blame me for my failed marriage placed me in a dark place. With time, I reasoned I could not blame them. Our social reality was different. Perhaps they came from family backgrounds where they had witnessed lots of sacrifices from their mothers to sustain their marriage which was completely different from my experience. My father died in his mid-thirties leaving behind a young, beautiful wife and mother to five children whose love for her deceased husband was alive every minute of her existence. Hence, she never entertained any thoughts of a second marriage.

In my process of adjustment to being single again, I realized I had not fully integrated myself back to South Africa after seven years of absence and schooling in Swaziland. Life in South Africa following those riots was far different from Swaziland. In fact, the apartheid policies had intensified. Casual congregations of people in street corners were avoided because they would draw negative attention and at times, led to police throwing tear gas to disperse them. By night time, streets were desolate. It was a risk to go out anytime of the day for fear of being hit by a stray bullet. Every day, massive arrests were taking place and most of those being arrested were innocent people. At the same time, there were young people joining underground freedom movements and going into self-exile. Life in exile was not safe either as there were reports of South Africa's Security Police infiltrating liberation movements in Botswana and Swaziland. It was during those years that one of the most admired leaders of the Black Consciousness Movement, Steve Biko lost his life in police custody. Such tragedies made life in South Africa uncertain and precarious. In the absence of alternatives, many people including myself, had to find a way to coexistence with the uncertainties of the time.

Since I had lived outside South Africa, I reasoned to myself, it would be physically and mentally liberating to be in Swaziland compared to being in South Africa, even if it were for just a weekend. Not only that, the social scene in Swaziland was much more open to one's choice compared to South Africa's restrictive measures of racial discrimination. If one wanted entertainment in South Africa, one could not go to White movie theaters or social clubs because of the Group Areas Act which barred Black South Africans from Whites only amenities. For Blacks, the best bet was to go to a tavern in the township commonly called a shebeen for entertainment. However, I never found them appealing. Being a woman and patronizing taverns in the townships was generally scorned. Faced with all these barriers I thought, I had relatives and old school mates in Swaziland who would be willing to accommodate me each weekend I was there. I can always go wherever I wanted to go. So, it made sense to me to take a taxi across the border every other Friday evening heading to Swaziland where I would spend Friday and Saturday nights with friends or relatives, then head back home Sunday afternoon, arriving at midnight. For the most part, passengers who were taking that trip did not know each other. So basically, the trips were with strangers and sometimes the same people did not make the same trips back to South Africa. The cab driver was the only one who knew every passenger. The driver also knew where each of his passengers lived. Hence, he had to make door to door deliveries on the return trips to South Africa.

One Friday afternoon, I picked up my ride at a central pick-up point at the Johannesburg train station. There were four passengers waiting when I arrived. We waited for a short while and were later joined by two more passengers. Shortly thereafter, we started boarding and left Johannesburg train station. The taxi was a mini-van which could accommodate six people and a driver, but not in a comfortable way when traveling for five hours. We had to go through border security clearances, the processing was uneventful. After the Oshoek border we made our way to Mbabane the capital of Swaziland. At that point, the delivery of passengers began, and I was among those being dropped off in Mbabane. Usually, on my arrival, my host would have lined up the itinerary for our weekend which involved going to the Royal Swazi Casino where most of the entertainment was. This was my favorite spot. Each time I visited this Casino I would be reminded of a memorable trip I made with my sister in our teenage years, to see Sarah Vaughn's first performance in Southern Africa. When it was time to get back to South Africa, as arranged, on Sunday afternoon, I got to the pickup point on time for my ride back to Johannesburg. On our arrival in Johannesburg, I was the second to be dropped off at my home. The taxi proceeded to drop off the rest of the passengers in other parts of Soweto.

It was in the early hours of a Wednesday morning at three a.m. to be precise when everyone in the house was awoken by what sounded like a thud. As Mother turned on the lights, approaching the front door, she asked, "Who is it?"

A gentle male voice responded in Zulu, "Yimina Mama special Branch." I could hear him clearly as I was right behind Mother. Mother and I looked at each other petrified. My two younger sisters stood by the bedroom door in panic. As Mother opened the door, a White male figure loomed in front of us, apologizing for what he described as 'an inconvenience'. As the White man entered the front of the house, I could see right behind him a Black man in handcuffs. Right behind him was an entourage of members of the South Africa's Special Branch. When I recognized who the Black man in handcuffs was, the taxi driver from my last trip to Swaziland, in my naivety, I called out his name asking, what happened. In a passive tone he responded, "Well, Sisi kubi" meaning, 'my sister, it is bad'. By that time, there were a number of Special Branch officers inside the house, searching every room while the 'front man' continued to convince Mother in Zulu, not to worry, explaining, all they need was for me to get dressed and come with them to answer a few questions at John Foster Square, the headquarters of South Africa's Special Branch. He promised I would be returned back home. I believed him and I was not scared. Rather, I was confident I had done nothing wrong.

Walking out of my home surrounded by security agents and police officers, I made several observations. There had been police officers with machine guns drawn surrounding the house. A convoy of six unmarked cars were parked outside my house. The handcuffed taxi driver was led to the first car. This became obvious to me that he was directing the Special Branch where to go. Afterall, he knew where each passenger from his previous ride lived. Secondly, we were purposely separated to avoid any contact. I was led to the second car with two security agents on either side of me in the back seat of the car. As the convoy pulled away from my home heading toward deep Soweto and not in the direction of their head office in Johannesburg, I said a prayer. I was awakening to the realization that this was the notorious early morning pickups by the South African Security Branch of suspected 'political insurgents' as they were called and I was one of them. My mother was fooled. I was not going to be back soon. I was going to John Forster Square for interrogation and most likely would never to be seen by my family ever again. Gripped by fear, my mind started racing as I tried to reflect on my previous visit to Swaziland. I asked myself, who had I met? Who had I talked to? What were the conversations about? Each time I drew a blank. By this time, it was daybreak, the convoy had made three more stops and was heading in the direction of Johannesburg. Upon arrival at John Forster Square, I was led to an elevator, from the elevator to a room and then ordered to sit. Two Afrikaans security men pulled their chairs up to sit, facing me at a distance of four feet, and began asking questions. Their green eyes piercing through mine, I began to sweat. In a quavering voice, I told them why I had gone to Swaziland. Who I stayed with? Who I met while in Swaziland? Who I rode with in the taxi?

Dissatisfied with my answers, they yelled out for someone in Afrikaans. Soon thereafter, a fellow about six foot tall wearing a thick black belt with a bunch of keys around his waist, walked in. He escorted me to another area of the building. As he reached for his keys, he opened a heavy steel door which led to my jail cell. Right there, it sank in that the promise made to my mother that I needed to answer a few questions and I would be returned back to the comfort of my home was a lie.

This cell could not have been more than eight by ten feet with a small window twenty feet high, a toilet bowl by the entrance door and next to it was a smelly, filthy sleeping area with a dark gray blanket. By this time, I was physically, mentally and emotionally worn out. I had lost my sense of time. I was sleepy. Afterall, I had

90

been up since three a.m. I was hungry but had no appetite. I had a lump in my throat. My head was spinning. Looking up toward those high windows, my eyes began to well with tears. I asked God, what had I done to deserve this experience. I thought about the pain my mother was going through not knowing my whereabouts. I had heard numerous stories of people who were hauled from their homes to John Forster Square never to be seen again. My hero, Steve Biko was one of them. Each time I revisit the events of that day, I shuddered to think how naïve I was to believe the Afrikaans man who convinced my mother I was being brought in to answer a few questions. Without a clock, watch or light in this cell, I could not tell what time it was until I heard the faraway shuffle accompanied by the openings and closures of cell doors coming closer to my cell. Finally, from a small opening at the bottom of the cell door, a covered stainless-steel plate was thrown in. From the smell of cabbage, I figured this to be my dinner but I had no appetite. As night fell, I could not face the darkness in this cell. My salvation was the light that shone through the small windows twenty feet above me.

Looking up toward those windows made me feel like I was still connected to the outside world. More importantly, I felt the connection with Mother's tears and my family. I have since experienced several memory lapses about that seven day stay in that cell.

However, I do remember going to sleep in my clothes for the entire seven days and never cleaning myself. Frankly, I could hardly sleep waiting for daybreak in hope that I would be freed. Each morning, I was awoken early in the morning, escorted to the elevator then to the interrogation room to be asked the same questions. Wrongful accusations were leveled against me for being a member of the underground political groups who were attempting to overthrow the South African regime. I listened to this brainwashing over and over again but I stood firm and refused to admit to something I did not do. Yet, over and over again they hoped to hear me say something different. Obviously frustrated with me, they yelled, cursed and threatened me. I stuck to my story. Whatever story they were looking for, it was not coming from me. I was simply sharing my truth about my trips to Swaziland.

By the fifth day of this back-and-forth interrogation sessions, a Black special branch officer was brought in to join the two Afrikaans officers. On this particular day, I was brought into the room. The Black interrogator asked me if I recognized him. He went on to tell me he knew my family well. He claimed to be related to one of our neighbors and frequented their residence. Once again, he wanted me to recount how I was connected to Swaziland beginning with the names and addresses of relatives and friends in Swaziland. After I finished, he brought a writing pad and pen to write everything I had just detailed to him, date and sign it. After I was done, I was escorted back to my cell. The following day, I was once more escorted to the high building office and told I was being released. I was driven in an unmarked car back to my home. A neighbor who saw me come out of the car, ran toward me screaming with joy. We embraced each other, walked toward my house and were met by my two sisters in tears. They told me Mother had been visiting every police station in Soweto after John Forster Square denied I was held there. She was out that particular day searching for my whereabouts. Once inside the house, the neighbor asked us to kneel down for a prayer. It was an emotional day. It became worse when Mother returned to find me back home.

In those days, anyone who had been arrested on suspicious involvement in the arms struggle to overthrow the South African regimes was ostracized by friends and the community out of fear. It was commonly believed that if you were to walk out of John Forster Square, someone had framed you or you had cut a deal with the Special Branch to be their spy. Because of my fragile mental state, I chose to distance myself from close friends. Luckily my job did not terminate me during my absence. I continued to work but kept to myself. I had no social life staying home every weekend. As I began to evaluate my life and my future within the context of South Africa, I came to the conclusion I needed to get out of South Africa. The idea that one could be imprisoned indefinitely without cause was inexcusable. It was a violation of one's basic human rights.

A year thereafter, I happened to walk past the taxi rank at the Johannesburg train station when I spotted the taxi driver who brought members of the South African Special Branch to my home. During those days, the area surrounding Johannesburg train station was clean and a safe area for a woman walking by herself. As I came closer to where the taxi driver was, I called out his name. He turned around, recognized me, waved and walked toward me. I noticed; his gait was different. He appeared to be limping. As he was approaching me, he was all smiles, extending his hand, all the while shaking his head. I surmised it was an expression of disbelief at seeing me, and recalling what he had done to my family by subjecting me to brutal interrogations and solitary confinement. As we stood there trying to articulate how we each felt, he apologized profusely for what my family was subjected to, noting that he did not have a choice. He went on to detail his experience at John Foster Square noting that at one point, he thought he was going to die. He admitted he was physically tortured. He noted that the South African government accused him of working for the underworld to enable anti-apartheid groups to smuggle guns to South Africa in order to destabilize the government. Further he detailed what had happened the day he was arrested. Seemingly, after he had dropped off all of his passengers including me from the trip to Swaziland, he was left with one passenger to drop off. It was about midnight when he arrived at the residence. He parked the car, pulled out the passenger's luggage and they both entered the gate heading toward the front door of the residence. As was his normal practice, he waited with the passenger while he opened the front door. Unbeknownst to both men, members of the South African Special Branch were hiding behind the bushes, in the front of the yard watching them. As they were ready to enter the house, they heard shuffles behind them and a group of men rushed toward them. For a while they thought they were being robbed. Soon they realized they were being accosted by White men some wearing police uniform, carrying machine guns. They were ordered to lay down on their stomachs. As they were being handcuffed, they were told they were under arrested. At that point they both realized this was no joke. They started recognizing there were both Black and White officers some in uniform speaking in Afrikaans. He stated, it was at that point when it registered to him, he literally knew nothing about this particular passenger nor any other passenger who had ridden with him across the South African border with Swaziland for all the years he had been operating his taxi service. He kept on reassuring himself that whatever came down, he would be exonerated

94

because he had done nothing illegal. Moreover, those who work at the Oshoek border post that separated South Africa from Swaziland knew him well and could attest to his clean reputation.

He proceeded to relate how they were escorted to John Forster Square, in Johannesburg, traveling in separate cars, driven by members of the special branch where they would be interrogated for several weeks. He could not remember the length of his stay there as he had lost contacts with the outside world. Because they were separated once they got to John Forster Square, he never saw the other passenger again. Following that lengthy interrogation which involved severe torture, he was accused of conspiracy to export weapons from Swaziland to blow up government buildings in South Africa. Only then did it register to him that by transporting passengers between the two countries he had placed himself and his business under precarious circumstances because of South Africa's political upheavals. From his account, it was not clear to me if he cut a deal with the South Africa's special branch when he led them back to Soweto to identify where he had dropped off his passengers that night. Since I happened to be amongst the first ones to be dropped off, I had no knowledge of who that passenger was and did not want to delve too much into their unfortunate past. Reportedly that last passenger's luggage was suitcases filled with explosives that had been received from anti-apartheid groups operating from Swaziland. The individual involved was also a member serving as a conduit between the South Africa based group with those who were operating outside the country and in this case, operating in Swaziland. Most troubling for these groups was the fact that they were infiltrated by spies, planted by South Africa's special branch. For example, this passenger was apprehended because of a tip that went to the South African special branch, alerting them about this person and his detailed traveling plans of arrival, location and the destructive weaponry he was bringing with him to South Africa for use in destabilizing South Africa's major operation sites. The taxi driver went on to explain that during those lengthy periods of interrogation, he pled for his innocence. However, he willingly agreed to help the Security Branch to round up all the passengers who were on that ride. The really sad part of this story is that the passenger who was arrested with him mysteriously died at John Forster Square. It was not known if he had a heart attack, had committed suicide or was murdered. All these revelations made me feel like I had been dually traumatized by not only spending seven days in solitary confinement for something I did not do, but also hearing the chilling accounts that we were actually riding in a taxi from Swaziland for five hours carrying dangerous explosives. Though traumatized, I was equally grateful to God for having my life spared.

After forty-eight years, I am still questioning the security system at the border. If indeed the car was loaded with dangerous weapons, they would have been detected at the Oshoek border post. All the trauma we experienced and a life lost would have been prevented. Overall, there was nothing rational about the massive arrests and the subsequent lives lost. As an aftermath of my solitary confinement, I became particularly anxious in crowded areas or in elevators. I began to pay close attention to the fear that often engulfed me whenever I was in crowded areas and tight spaces like elevators. Noticeably, I developed a new fear of visiting caves. As a child, I loved going to the caves. I was first introduced to caves when I was eight years old. A local

YMCA used to organize annual New Year's picnics for children from Soweto to Magaliesburg which is an hour's drive from Soweto. This town had rivers, farms and mountains. One of the attractions of Magaliesburg were the caves from the old mines.

Though not clinically diagnosed with claustrophobia, in one of my visits to my late father's family in Port Shepstone a cousin booked my youngest sister and I on an overnight premier class train from Johannesburg to Durban perhaps a lower grade of luxurious train travel in comparison to the blue train. The excitement of boarding a train for an overnight travel to Durban took me back to my later years in boarding school when as teenagers, our parents felt we were old and responsible enough to travel by ourselves by train to Swaziland. That evening, my sister and I watched through our windows the scenic and not so scenic views of the countryside as the train meandered past old towns while reminiscing about our childhood. When the porter came to arrange for our bedding, it was time for dinner. By the time we returned to our compartment, it was getting dark and we had to close the compartment door and the windows. The compartment space became much tighter. I was gripped with anxiety. I felt I was losing my mind. I stood up, began to gasp for air. Petrified, my sister asked if I was okay. Of course, I was not. Frankly I did not know what was happening to me. I asked her if we could keep the windows half opened for air and not turn off the lights. By the look on her face, she was puzzled and annoyed because she wanted to go to sleep. She wanted the lights out. She laid herself down and turned her back on me as I sat there on my bed with my face sticking out of the window. To be clear, in addition our age difference of seven years, we had not been in each other's company this close in a long time. So, it came as no surprise that she would be less sensitive to me. At some point, I had to close the window because of the cold air but kept the shutters open. As I sat on that bed, rummaging through my thoughts, trying to figure out what was going on with me, I finally realized this was the impact of that twenty-seven-year-old trauma I had experienced while in solitary confinement.

VIII

LOSING A MOTHER AND WELCOMING A NEW LIFE

Feeling ostracized from friends following my release from solitary confinement, I chose to avoid any types of socializing and turned down invitations to public events. Going to work and keeping myself busy at home was my refuge. Bad choices, are simply bad choices. No one forces you to do anything but sometimes life thrusts you in situations you regret for the rest of your life. On one of those lonely Saturday afternoons I accepted an invitation to a party from someone who was friends with my sister's boyfriend. To this day, I cringe at the thought of allowing my vulnerability to lead me to a disastrous relationship. A year later, I became a mother to a precious daughter. Motherhood came to me under unusual circumstances. Regardless, I was prepared to make major sacrifices to protect her. This included not yielding to any pressures of a marriage or a continuation of a relationship. While these choices tended to look selfish to others, they were the right decisions for our future. I made a promise then that I would do whatever it took to give her a new life elsewhere, away from a country that offered no prospects for a brighter future. It was during those months of nursing my seven-month-old baby that I lost the pillar of my strength. The devastation of losing a mother was not something I had expected. She labored so hard for her five children following the untimely death of a husband she loved so dearly. Throughout her years as a widow, and a mother of five, she took her role as a single parent with honor. Though she had suitors, having lost her husband when she was thirty-four years old, she constantly reminded us that being a single mother was a choice she had made out of love for her deceased husband. More importantly, she wanted to retain her husband's last name until she died. Sis' Tutu as she was commonly addressed by people in the neighborhood, conducted herself with much grace. From sharing a bag of potatoes with neighbors or her special Christmas pudding during the holidays with her neighbors and family members, everything she did was done with a gentle spirit and caring for others. Every day when she returned home from work, she would pull out of her pocketbook, a banana, an apple and an orange that she had saved from her lunch meal at the hospital, to share it with her five children. It became customary for all five of us to get a piece of an apple, banana and an orange every day. Mother sacrificed so much to ensure that her children had an education and a decent life. Now she had taken her last breath before her retirement. Where is the fairness in life? Selfishly, my mind drifted to the time that she intervened in what could have been a fatal attack on one of our neighbors. Mother begged the young man who was running berserk after a frightened neighbor on his property, wielding a knife, accusing the neighbor of defrauding him. Indeed, he was saved once again after so many similar situations with people accusing him of all kinds of scams, and scared girlfriends banging on our door in the middle of the night because he was threatening to assault them. Mother always came to his rescue. God took the good ones and left bad ones.

The day I got that unforgettable telephone call, I was alone in the house with my baby. I had visited Mother the previous day. On that day of the visit, as I was approaching the entrance of the hospital, I bumped into my sister on her way out. She was in a hurry. I remember her saying her driver was waiting in the car since she was on an assignment to cover a story. When I walked to Mother's bed, she was on an oxygen machine. As I stood there in tears, a nurse approached me with no explanation but politely asked me to leave. I was confused, but realized I might never see her again. As I walked down the hilly side of General Hospital, in the Hillbrow section of Johannesburg, toward the train station, on my way to Soweto, I saw my world closing in. I could not stop crying. At the same time, I felt as if Mother was feeling my pain. I felt like she was reassuring me that we would all be all right. Since I was in deep thoughts I did not even realize that the train was approaching my destination. When I arrived home, I walked around the house asking myself, what next?

I was just about to turn on the electric kettle to make tea when the telephone rang. My hands were trembling when I picked up the receiver. The voice on the other side relayed the message that Florence Balakazi Nxumalo passed away at six p.m. South African time. What followed thereafter, I still cannot remember. I know I hung up the phone, ran to a neighbor's house, screaming. The neighbor came out of her house. She reached out to me, hugged me and led me back to my home. Mother had passed away following complications from an exploratory brain surgery to remove a clot in her brain. Such medical procedures were new in South Africa and mostly performed by young White surgeons with little experience. It was widely known that to boost their credentials, White surgeons tended to perform more and unnecessary procedures on Black patients. Also, the common perception was that Black South Africans were their guinea pigs. In those days, one could not sue for medical malpractice. At least in my world, it was unheard of. Her death certificate registered 'death due to pneumonia'.

She had been told several times that the clot in her brain had to be removed, but she refused to grant permission. A registered nurse by profession, her refusal was not out of ignorance. It was out of fear of medical negligence and the wide spread medical experimental procedures performed on patients which often ultimately led to fatal outcomes. Unfortunately, her condition was deteriorating significantly. She had lost her balance and could not stand without falling. Her speech was becoming impaired. During one of my regular hospital visits, a nurse approached me to express her concerns about Mother's condition. She pleaded with me to talk to Mother and convince her to go for surgery. I felt terribly overburdened because I knew she did not want the surgery, yet the reality was that she was not getting any better. Out of desperation, I sat down with her to process what was happening to her. I asked her how she was feeling. She shook her head and looked down as if she was coming to grips with her condition. I then asked if she was still opposed to getting surgery to remove the clot. She looked at me like a scared child and asked me, "What should I do, Joey?" Tears welling down my face, I told her I was just concerned because she was not getting better. She nodded her head in agreement. She said, "Sign the papers, Joey."

Soon after those papers were signed, she was transported to Baragwanath hospital in Soweto where the surgery was performed. I visited her the day before the surgery and after the surgery had been done. On the day following her surgery, I entered her ward but I did not recognize the person laying on that bed. I walked out of the ward to find the nurse in charge. As soon as I spotted the nurse, I walked toward her to find out if Mother had returned from surgery and if so, where she was. She pointed me back to where I was when I came in. I went back to that ward but Mother was unrecognizable. Her face was swollen, hence I had walked past her bed, because I could not recognize that face. The same nurse approached me. She politely asked me to give her time to rest. She suggested that the following day might be a better day to visit with her. Indeed, I left the hospital to returned the following day. The following day, I was told she had been transported back to Johannesburg General Hospital for her recuperation. Not suspecting there was anything amiss but feeling encouraged, the next day I made the trip to Johannesburg General Hospital. Once at the hospital, I was directed to her ward. Needless to say, that finding her plugged into an oxygen machine was not expected and quite shocking. I had hardly been there for three minutes when I was subsequently asked to leave by the nurse in charge. I tried to ask questions but she was not willing to answer. I stood there at the end of her bed feeling helpless and distraught. The nurse walked up to me again insisting that I leave. Finally, I left the ward crying. Was I surprised? Not at all. In all actuality, this was typical of South Africa and how Black family members of patients were treated. Doctors lacked bed side manners. They were never accessible. They rarely honored Black family members' request for explanations. Could it be that because we were Black, we were not entitled to the courtesy of knowing what was happening to a loved one? I walked out of that hospital dejected, crushed, feeling like my world was closing in on me. My mind racing with rhetorical questions, 'will she recover?' "Why is she on an oxygen machine?' Mother was one of them. She was part of those professional teams of doctors, nurses who toiled nights and days to take care of patients unconditionally. She did not deserve this type of cold treatment. Taking care of her patients was her passion to the extent that each day she lost a patient, as her children, we got to know a part of that patient's story. This was her way of letting go and grieving their loss.

Given South Africa's history of negligence and secrecy in their medical practices and abuses when it came to Black patients' rights to know, as well as of their next of kin, my family stayed uninformed until Mother's medical certificate was released. Some of the details were revealed by one of the nursing sisters who came to pay her respects to the family. It was through her that the family came to know that Mother's surgery did not go well. Further, she informed us that the reason she was sent back to General Hospital was for her to receive her comfort care. Yet, the family was never notified. The family did contemplate on seeking legal counseling but such decisions were never formalized. Most likely there was also the realization that such legal actions are rarely done and that they were costly. To this day, I believe her case is one of many medical malpractices on Black patients in South Africa by White physicians that will remain uninvestigated for justifiable interventions. It symbolizes one of South Africa's most atrocious health care system failures for a country that was once one of the leaders of medical advancement in Southern Africa.

Mother had one of the most dignified and memorable burial service I can remember. The day of her funeral was a pleasant, sunny, early autumn day with clear skies. Family, friends and her co-workers had assembled at the Holy Cross Anglican Church to pay their last respects. At the end of the service, as the casket was being escorted out of the church with family leading the procession, the sky suddenly opened up with a slight sprinkle of rain, somewhat symbolic of our tears. One could see at the horizon, a beautiful rainbow lighting the skies, and just as suddenly the rain stopped. Once we got to the cemetery and the stainless-steel casket which my sister and her ex-husband purchased was lowered into the ground, I suddenly felt overcome by a spirit of comfort as I visualized her warm sincere smile as she was bidding us farewell. Mother's graceful send-off not only represented her character and dignity but it was also indicative of her humble spirit of coexistence with others, always seeking harmony with others. The choice of Mother's stainless-steel casket was symbolic of the 'dream car' she always imagined herself driving, a silver Mercedes Benz which incidentally, she would not have driven because she did not drive.

Mother's death signaled the beginning to a chapter of self-reflection and a period of long-term decision-making for us, as her children, to begin charting our own paths as self-governing individuals. No longer could we rely on her presence for that emotional, mental and physical security. This was the true beginning of self-reliance. Luckily for me, those plans had been stuck in the pipeline since the day I walked out of that solitary confinement. I purposely prolonged it for fear of leaving Mother behind and out of the need to be there for her should anything happen to her. Now that she was gone, I had to think through my future plans but this time not for myself alone, but for my baby as well. The amazing thing is that I was not afraid or hesitant, but completely determined to make it whatever it cost.

The country that protected me, gave me an identity despite the oppression, was no longer a safe place for me. It was becoming a dangerous country. Government policies which had entrenched racial divisions were now becoming reckless with no mercy for Black people, young, old, educated, wealthy, poor or law abiding. In the government's eyes all Black people had no loyalty to the country. The constant question I asked myself was, what future will my child have in this country? The little freedom Black people had could be taken away at the drop of a hat. How or why then would I hope for change? Economic sanctions imposed against South Africa by western countries in the 1970s failed to bring any relief for Black South Africans. Instead, Soweto was turning into a Lebanon with armored military trucks patrolling the streets, day in and day out. The fear of being hit by a stray bullet kept everyone indoors. In fact, news coverages of people hit by stray bullets became a sensation. I became convinced, I had to make a move soon. Those words from my parents to widen our horizon and think of a future beyond the confines of a brutal regime resonated with me. Indeed, the world was wide open for everyone to explore. That seed had been planted years ago. Now it was up to me to realize it. I began seeking out opportunities to further my studies abroad. I started networking with old college mates, friends who had traveled abroad, I visited libraries. One of the great things I admired about my people then was the spirit of sharing information. People were eager and willing to help as long as one expressed an interest to further one's education.

IX

TRANSNATIONAL EXPERIENCE

It is a marvel to arrive at a point in life whereby a day, an hour, a moment is simply a time to treasure. It is no surprise that no one tells you exactly when it will manifest itself nor how it will come. Undoubtedly, when it comes, suddenly there is that realization that you are where you were supposed to be. It is gradually unfolding right in front of you. It is happening. It is unexplainable. Maybe there is no need to explain it because it is of your own doing. Unbeknownst to you, you are actually the architect of the experience. Little do you realize that over time, you have been creating, shaping and influencing your world to be what it is at that moment. As you take stock of all notable gurus you have listened to and their account about our universe and how it can be manipulated to our benefit, you begin to appreciate the enlightenment. In the quest of the over-exaggerated, elusive concept of happiness, you have tried the 'how to' approaches espoused by renowned gurus which at times only related to a fraction of where you wanted to be, not where you were at the time. Whenever that happened, you felt cheated, and became even more disillusioned. You were overcome by impatience, anger and the urge for quick fixes which often times, left you in total despair. Suddenly, you realized that happiness is not universal nor a common entity. It is what one makes of it. Only at this moment you realize that perhaps happiness is not mutually inclusive with self-discovery or personal success. You become fully aware that the wealth of knowledge amassed over the years, and the pitfalls you encountered along the journey, they were actually the engines to today's life. There comes a realization that contentment is entwined with these experiences.

Each and every one of us goes through life's journey which often times seem unending. It's a journey that takes us through valleys and quagmires. Despite fleeting moments of happiness, we might experience along the way that the 'it' of our existence constantly eludes us. Often times, we see ourselves as not measuring up to society's standards or to those standards set by family and peers. Invariably, self-doubt sets in. Yet, a silent voice beckons us to move on in pursuit of 'it' and to discover ourselves. Indeed, we move on. Opportunities come along; taking us to countries and to people we never imagined we would ever see in our life time. This is a journey I experienced as I entered my thirties.

The first opportunity for me to experience the outside world far beyond the oceans came out of Stuttgart, Germany. I had never heard of Stuttgart. Also, the thought of learning a new language similar to that of my oppressor; Afrikaans, was unsettling. According to a co-worker who was friends with my college classmate who had moved to Stuttgart, life for foreigners was not good. One felt like an outsider, with language barriers exacerbating the challenges for foreigners. I also knew I needed to stay within my career field and not attempt to start on a new discipline. In a way, it became easy not to pursue that scholarship. There were many factors stacked against me going to Germany. English speaking countries were much preferred, mostly opportunities in America.

I began to seriously consider the opportunity of going to America. Quite often, the United States Consulate Offices in Johannesburg would announce educational opportunities to study or participate in professional development programs in the United States. Such opportunities would be in different disciplines. As a result, a number of individuals I knew were able to further their studies in the United States. Again, one would learn about these opportunities by word of mouth. There were other similar opportunities through other countries as well. However, the United States was the one favored by many of my generation. My passage to the United States came through one of these opportunities and landed me in the southern part of the United States. I loved everything about the Carolinas. The gentle nature of the people and the overall slow pace of life was so enlightening with my preference for nature of country living rather than city living. I had seen New York when I arrived in the United States and I knew right away, I would never live there. New York was too overwhelming. People in New York were fast talkers and because of the American accent, I could hardly understand what they were saying. Perhaps it was the way people in the South articulated that was to me, fascinating. I felt I could live in the South forever. I have to admit, at the beginning I had no idea of America's social injustices. I was blinded by my ignorance. My overall knowledge of the United States' history was very shallow and fragmented. It was never taught where I came from nor did I make it my priority to learn about it on my own. In certain instances, I would get snippets of information about the United States' history, mostly about slavery when I was on a visit to Uncle George's place. Uncle George often hosted his friends who were all teachers in Swaziland and they would engage in these intellectual discussions to equate apartheid to Jim

Crow's laws in America. So, my knowledge of America's history was quite limited.

I remembered that when we were young, after my father's death, Mother often communicated with an American family. Reportedly, this family knew my father from his travels abroad and had been in touch with Mother providing her with financial support whenever they could, following my father's death. They had girls about our age and would send us packages full of clothing. However, with time, communications ceased. We never heard from them and Mother did not receive any responses to her correspondence. On my arrival to the US, I thought about them and wondered how I would locate them. Luckily, I had two young families who graciously offered to be my host families, a White family and a Black family. My first host family was the White couple. They were educated, well-read about South Africa and very kind. I recall that they were expecting their first child. They had neighbors, an elderly couple who were quite pleasant, but somewhat limited in terms of current events, to include politics of the Southern African region. One afternoon, I was outside in the backyard with my host family and the neighbors came out to introduce themselves to me. I can remember the first question coming out of the elderly woman's mouth which I found unflattering was, "Oh! Did you get those clothes in New York on your arrival to the United States? Do you eat rice in your country?"

It hit me. "Yes I am from Africa and that is how we are perceived by the western world as savages." I was stunned not only at the ignorance but at the audacity of suggesting I must have been naked when I stepped off a plane from South Africa to have bought my clothes in New York. I contemplated on my response and thought, maybe I should use the opportunity as a teaching moment to share with her where I came from, not necessarily to talk about the geographic location of South Africa on the map, but to highlight the social and political structure of my country. I decided not to, but to simply smile instead. At that moment, the hosting couple gently shared a brief background with them about my country, making sure that the elderly couple understood that South Africa was a separate country in Africa, and that it practiced apartheid which they equated to Jim Crow laws. Their response left me dumbfounded. The neighbor's wife simply retorted, "Oh honey, we do not have that here. Here, it is the green, the mighty dollar," meaning there is no racism in the US but it is all about socio-economics. Such words signaled to me ignorance and denial about America's history of slavery. Unable to reasonably respond to that explanation, the conversation came to an abrupt end.

It so happened that my hosting couple both graduated from the university I was going to attend. I expressed to them how thrilled I was to have been accepted at their alma mater, a highly rated university in the South. They assured me I was going to have the best educational experience there and meet foreign students from all over the world. Indeed, it turned out that coming to this university made it possible for me to meet students from other African countries. As members of the African Student Organization we had regular meetings to address issues that were unique to us coming from Africa and adjusting to the American culture. In addition, we were able to gain a greater understanding about America's immigration laws and their impact on us should we decide to stay after out graduation. Mingling with other African students was an eye opener because Black South

Africans had close to no contacts with other Africans. Apartheid laws barred any travels for members of the Black population to most of the African countries. However, laws were very flexible for travels to the former British Protectorates such as Swaziland, Botswana and Lesotho. Through these meetings we got to learn a lot about each other, good and bad. It was during such gatherings that one got to know how Black South Africans were perceived by their brothers and sisters in the rest of Africa. Basically, what I learned from these interactions with fellow Africans was that we were despised for subordinating ourselves to a minority White population. Such simplistic accusations made it look like we had a choice or control over the oppressive regime. Sadly, any attempts to explain the sheer power of economics and politics that White South Africans enjoyed in comparison to Black South Africans, were ignored, dismissed and ridiculed. Yet these were the same countries that lost so much of their mineral wealth during colonization. By the time they gained independence, they had to rely on the west for skills and capital to function as independent countries. It was very disheartening to listen to the disparaging things they would say about Black South Africans. Yet, stories coming out of exiled South Africans who had spent years living in those African countries were not flattering. They painted a much dreamier picture of their supposedly, 'free countries'. The arrogance, lack of empathy and disdain they demonstrated toward my people, some of whom had died for trying to right the country's injustices left me empty and disappointed. I asked myself, what was I missing? As recollected by a South African who went into exile and stayed in different African countries; life was miserable in those countries compared to the life they had left in South Africa. Grass was not as green as they had anticipated. They shared sad accounts of having to line up early in the morning to receive a ration for basic foods like bread, milk, salt. Listening to these stories, it never sounded like such an existence represented countries I would consider as better than where I was raised. Besides, whereas South Africans who completed their studies abroad, particularly men were very eager to go back to South Africa compared to my other brothers from the continent. In fact, in one of the colloquia held by the entire student organization, and led by a White American political science student to explore the dichotomy of a liberated and a non-liberated African man in the context of Africa, he used Black South Africans as an example of a non-liberated African man. One of the questions that he raised which piqued my interest was related to an observation of African men who came from once colonized countries but were now in liberated African countries. However, once they completed their studies abroad, opted out of going back to their native countries to plough back their knowledge and skills. Yet, Black South African men though still living under a White oppressive regime, once they completed their studies abroad, they returned back to their native country. Frankly, it was enlightening to listen to those ensuing discussions. I recall an observation shared by one attendee at this colloquium who was in agreement that Black South Africans men whenever they went abroad to study, they always returned back to their country. He wondered aloud if it had anything to do with the knowledge that their country had mineral wealth and a stable economy in comparison to the rest of the Southern African region. Though this wealth was in the hands of the minority White South Africans, Black South Africans were also optimistic of prospects of a better future, despite the hostile and chaotic political climate which robbed Black South Africans of their human rights.

Another point raised was the fact that Black South Africans faced numerous restrictions in terms of free movement. They could not freely travel outside the country except to neighboring countries like Botswana, Lesotho and Swaziland. Hence, they grew up knowing absolutely nothing about Kenya, Ghana, Nigeria other than from news reports, books or personal accounts from those who were in exile. This type of isolation from self-ruling African nations was not a mistake. It was by design, typical of the framework that was used in South Africa to divide and rule. So, the majority of Black South Africans knew little about the state of other African countries beyond the fact that most gained self-rule, thus were free from any bondage still suffered by Black South Africans. Yet we were not considered "brothers" because as Black South Africans we had supposedly shamed the rest of Africa for allowing a minority White population to rule South Africa, a simplistic view for a complex situation. Some of these individuals who were vocal at these meetings were well-respected intellectuals who had studied elsewhere in Europe, typical of what I call career students. It is an irony that forty years thereafter, these are the same people descending on South Africa in multitudes claiming South Africa as belonging to the rest of Africa, therefore their rightful country as well. Not only that, some of them brought corruption, fraud, human trafficking, drugs, child bride practices and an overall life-style that was not only contrary to traditional practices for South Africans but foreign to South Africa's rule of law. While polygamy was prevalent and practiced in rural areas, there was always tension between these practices and the strongly held Christian beliefs. South Africa had its own challenges spanning the apartheid era. However, what has since happened in South Africa is tragic. The country's social and economic structures have been overburdened by the external problems of neighboring countries, not to the exclusion of corruption by its government officials. The moral fiber is in disarray. It is primarily driven by greed, drugs.

It was at these meetings that I had a chance encounter of meeting an African American brother. It seemed like the universe had aligned our energies together. His looks resembled those of a Teddy Pendergrass or an Isaac Hayes that some Black South African women idolized, me included. Proud of his heritage and eager to know more about the brothers and sisters from the 'mother land', he was friendly, eloquent and affable. He seemed extremely comfortable with the group and keen to know more about them. As he began to ask me about South Africa, he somewhat bragged about knowing a lot about South Africa from watching Shaka Zulu movies, listening to Miriam Makeba's click songs and from reading Alan Paton's book, *Cry the Beloved Country*. He threw words here and there like Sophia town, Soweto and Johannesburg. Needless to say, I was completely swept away and there was a reason for it. Up until that time, it seemed like very few African Americans knew as much about South Africa as he did, more importantly, about the experiences of Black South Africans, except for my second host family who were African Americans and well-vested in South African anti-apartheid and the divestment movement of the 1960s. With time, I got to know more about him. He was drafted at seventeen years old to go and serve his country during the Vietnam War. I admired everything about him. A year thereafter, I married the man who constantly reminded me that of outmost importance, he was a proud American before being Black. I came to accept and admire his patriotism. This was a man who indulged in eclectic music collections and could not be pigeon-holed into any stereotypical categories. Bruce Springsteen, Joan Baez, Tootsie and the Maytals, Leonard Cohen, Joni Mitchell and Clarence Carter were part of his favorite collection. Though I grew to love all of his collection, the musicians were foreign to me. He sparked my interest and curiosity in so many other things that I had never heard of like his elaborate discussions about horsepower in cars to the abstract structural make ups of the Sunshine Skyway Bridge in St. Pietersburg, Florida. We learned a lot from each other. He teased me a lot about my pronunciations and I would tease him back about his. We shared a lot in common and had great laughs at our cultural differences. However, there were small things that were unsettling. His constant utterances of damn this… F— his, Mo… This, made me shudder. I was not used to that type of language. Such expressions were not only new to me but they were appalling. I took them personally. However, he never saw anything wrong or distasteful about them because to him this was America, take it or leave it. For me, this was tough medicine to swallow. The cross-cultural experience had a different twist and was full of surprises. While friends of mine from South Africa used to be envious to learn that he cooked (only on my birthday and Mother's Day), washed dishes, bought groceries quite often and helped the kids with homework when I was not available to do it, most of these chores were performed by women in South Africa. Men found it demeaning to their manhood to perform some of these chores. Our areas of conflict centered around problem-solving skills. Whereas I preferred to discuss our points of differences, he could not do it without major escalations. I came to realize later that he bottled up a lot of his emotions and when he could no longer do it, he would explode. I attributed his challenges to his traumatic experiences in Vietnam at a young age, without getting professional attention

116

upon his discharge.

Pursuing graduate studies while raising a family was not an easy task. There were major demands on both of us. We were both over-extended. He was working two jobs to support a family, while I worked part-time at a library while attending classes at night and on Saturdays. Hence, after passing my comprehensive exams and working on my dissertation, it became imperative that I got a job to relieve him of the family's financial burdens. He became my strong pillar as I negotiated the tough terrain of higher education while finishing my dissertation and defending it. My first teaching position in Florida proved to be my greatest challenge. When I was interviewed for the position at this private college, I learned I would be the second Black faculty member in the entire college. Because of my warped impression of America, I did not think any further about the impact nor long term consequences of it. All I was excited about was to finally put my foot in the door. The day I reported for the school's academic opening day I was informed that the other Black faculty member had resigned. I began to formulate a real picture of what I was walking into in terms of the work climate. The majority of students were White. There were a few Black students a majority of whom were from the islands and athletes. I befriended an Administrative Assistant who worked in the Dean's office, an intelligent well-spoken, Black woman with a British-Caribbean accent. We somehow took a liking to each other and became best friends. She had worked at this university for some time and knew a lot about the politics of the school and the heavy pockets of some of these students' parents. I received a lot of schooling on the dos and don'ts. I was also fortunate to have two mentors, a male colleague in my program who was such a kind and reassuring person who, whenever I doubted myself, would uplift my spirits and remind me; teaching is an art, it comes with practice. It does not happen overnight. No matter how much you try, there will be students who will make you feel inadequate. However, if you understand group dynamics and the power struggles that ensues in a group, the defense mechanisms that are likely at play with certain students who are trying to hide their short-comings, you will understand you are going through a test. It became clear to me that indeed, there were individual students who demonstrated a lack of adequate preparation for college. I then thought, perhaps to acknowledge that they needed help from someone, who was a teacher but still a foreigner, was difficult for them. Most of these students were eloquent speakers but when it came to their writing they made careless errors. My second mentor was a smart, strong woman who headed our department of Social Sciences. They both shielded me from unkind criticisms and scrutiny from two colleagues. These colleagues, a man and a woman were vicious. In addition to condescending comments, they would make whenever they saw me in the hallways or at a meeting, they took pleasure in standing outside my classroom door while I was delivering a lecture, just to spite me. I had never seen such lack of integrity and unprofessionalism. I withstood all that harassment and remained unfazed by it. Given my accent, maybe they were curious to hear how I sounded in a lecture though I had given a lecture during my hiring process. I was very careful not to equate their behavior to that of some White people in South Africa who took pride in getting as low as they could to belittle and push someone who was 'not of their kind' out of the door. Given my naivety about America, this type of behavior was unexpected and quite shocking.

I like sharing a story with my current students about my first salary after I was hired at this university in Florida. I have shared this story quite often as a way of encouraging students to consider other aspects of a career job that will fulfil them beyond a salary. When I was hired for this teaching job, I was considered as having an ABD which stands for All But a Degree. This was due to the fact that I had not yet completed my dissertation to earn my PhD degree. As a result, I was hired as an instructor pending the conferring of my degree. After I received my degree, I was promoted to assistant professor. The salary difference from instructor to assistant professor was a mere $1000.00. I used this example every time when my students would complain about a salary offer, they had received. Needless to say, they could not believe I had my terminal degree yet I was offered a pittance of a salary from $20,000 per year to $21,000 a year. So, in addition to the indignations, I had experienced in that current job, in a country that I loved so much and respected for what it stood for to us in South Africa, I was not paid for what I was worth. Basically, I was exploited and perhaps to discourage me from staying. The combination of the two led me to explore other options. After teaching for two years, and suffocating in that demeaning environment, I made a move which allowed me to be with my young children after-school, and during summer breaks. Despite the unhealthy work environment, I walked away having learned quite a lot about academia.

The next job I secured after leaving that first teaching job was with a local county's board of education. I was hired as a school social worker. This job paid me what I was worth. The working conditions were the best I could ever dream of under a supervisor who nurtured all of the twelve workers under him, equally. He fostered a working environment of responsibility, quality, integrity, transparency and collaboration. He recognized the heavy demands of the job at a time when families were disintegrating due to the prevalence of crack cocaine leading to domestic violence, absenteeism, child abuse and negligence and high incarceration rates. It was the first time in my nine years of practice that I felt so proud of my profession and the people I worked with for the passion they exuded and the long hours they spent in the office, particularly on Fridays to make sure all case entries were completed. Though a move to Florida had paid off, for both of us, when my ex-husband's company relocated him to the Northeast, it became time for me too to start looking for another job again. However, I had to stay behind for another four months with the children so they could finish off their school year. Also, I had to complete my year's contract. During this time, I had earnestly started to look for another job, a third one to be precise. I used my networking groups to get back to academia and search for teaching positions in the Northeast. I had kept in touch with a classmate from my doctoral program who was already teaching and heavily involved in our professional organization. In fact, we had presented at one of their conferences as doctoral students. She encouraged me to attend their annual conference which I did. I went through the conference job announcement board and decided to meet with representatives from the university who were recruiting for faculty. I met with them and I was advised to send in my resume and additional documents. I returned home and a week thereafter I got a call inviting me for an interview with the rest of their faculty and students. I experienced a high level of anxiety. Meanwhile, my then spouse was trying to discourage me from going for the interview. His rationale was the distance. To him, it made no sense to go for the interview because if I were to be hired, I would have to deal with the long commute of an hour and thirty minutes from where we had planned to settle. He had chosen that location because the public school system was good. I was unswayed. I told him, as a foreigner, it was an honor, a privilege, to be invited for an interview and therefore I was going and would deal with the outcome. I had been to interviews before but none of the others felt so good during or after. I felt like I was engaging in conversations of curiosity and mutual interests with peers and students in a non-intimidating manner. Color was not a significant factor. Out of eight people in that room including students, only two were Black, myself and one member of faculty. Leaving that interview room, I was walking on cloud nine. I met up with my ex-husband who had been waiting inside their guest room. He asked, "How did it go," I told him, I did not know but I was feeling good about the interview. Driving back to the hotel, I had to listen attentively to his lecture about highway driving in the state and on and on about state troopers. I explained to him that I had already been warned by others on how to drive in the Northeast.

This new job in the Northeast proved to be quite different from the one I had in Florida, so I thought. In fact when my previous colleagues threw a farewell party for me, those who had migrated from the Northeast to Florida began preparing me for what they described as a huge adjustment. The first one was that 'Northerners are not as friendly as the Southerners'. The second advice was, 'for the most part they do not mean what they say' and lastly, 'you have to learn to be a defensive driver because they are terrible drivers'. I took the advice in great strides telling myself, moving from South Africa to America was a huge adjustment. This change from the South to the North was not going to be that big of a deal. I felt like I had found a niche at this university. People were extremely supportive. They were advising me to join committees, to participate in university-wide activities and university committees for visibility. They offered to observe my teaching so I could receive feedback and make improvements where necessary. I was also matched with two mentors from outside my department. I worked extremely well with my department mentor. She made sure that I was exposed to the university community by joining different committees and being involved with key colleagues to help me navigate the tenure process. Once our career paths seemed stabilized, we began discussing plans to take a trip to South Africa. As the days grew closer to our departure date my daughters' excitement of visiting their mother's birthplace seemed to be cooling down. Instead, it was replaced by lots of excitement over visiting my cousins in London. I was mystified by the sudden change of attitude toward going to South Africa but I let it play itself out. I was also aware that their dad had been sitting them down to watch South African movies, to somewhat prepare them for the trip. I wondered aloud if somehow a few of the movies they had watched were confusing to them as they covered barbaric content of naked warriors in the jungle, wielding spears. For instance, did they have reservations about visiting their mother's birth place for fear it was in a jungle? If so, were they concerned about how to adjust to whatever that environment looked like? I was quite amused by the thought that my children could be worried about their survival in their mother's homeland, yet again, we are all petrified by the unknown.

The day we boarded the British airway flight to London, I

watched my daughters walk briskly with their radio headphones on, each one wheeling her own carry-on suitcase, wearing their blue jean outfits, an attire we all chose to wear for its convenience. On our first leg of our trip, we visited my first cousins who were based in London in self-exile. One studied and lived in London and the other one lived in Birmingham. I can recall the excitement written all over my daughters' faces as we landed at Heathrow airport. We checked out of customs. My ex had to find a car rental for a car to use throughout our five day stay in London. Everything worked out smoothly. We packed our luggage in the rental car all excited and began to navigate ourselves out of the airport to the center of London. The girls kept on cautioning their dad to drive on the other side of the road because he was on the wrong side. As expected, he retorted, "I know how to drive. I'm on the right side of the road." To his credit, he quickly realized he was not by that time, he had run into traffic cones. It was hilarious. The girls' excitement of being in London was uncontrollable. They wanted to go to a McDonald at Trafalgar Square and to see Harrods. We assured them; we would go to McDonalds because Harrods was beyond our league. It was completely out of the question. We were not, by any stretch of imagination the types of people to even walk-through Harrods' doors. McDonalds on Trafalgar Square was not like anything we were familiar with in the US. Finally, we made our way to the friend's house in the center of London, a pricey house for the size of the structure and almost nothing around its yard. Again, this was London. For the rest of our four days stay, we visited my cousins, went to see the houses of Parliament building.

The most telling experience about my daughters' feelings of going to South Africa was on the eve of our departure for the second leg of the trip. Their chattiness diminished. At the table during dinner they were uncommunicative and appeared morose. Our host's wife asked if everything was OK, their response was incoherent. As she was probing to find out if anything was wrong, they stood up, excused themselves, stating they needed to finish packing. As they left the dining room where we had all been sitting, in a whisper I explained to our hosts what I suspected was their source of anxiety. They found it hilarious. They were amused because though born in London, their parents were from Jamaica and had gone through the same experience with their son when he visited Jamaica for the first time.

Our flight from Heathrow airport in London to Johannesburg's Jan Smuts Airport was uneventful as it was an evening flight. They watched a few on-flight movies and fell asleep. They were up by the time the air hostess came around to serve breakfast. At landing, their eyes were everywhere to see whatever they were curious to see. As we exited customs, family members were there to meet us. It was all excitement and a realization on my daughters' part that, after all, this was not some kind of a jungle. Their eyes lit up as the car passed the hilly parts of Johannesburg to Illovo where we spent a couple of days at my sister's place. Their demeanor had changed completely. They were eager to see the rest of South Africa which was impossible given the two weeks we had at our disposal. However, we were able to take short drives around the city, from the wealthy suburbs to the poorest areas. They were keen to go to malls but unfortunately, they were told malls were not part of our itinerary. I had emphasized to my ex-husband that our first item of business on our arrival was to allow my family to perform a traditional welcoming ceremony and once it was done, we would be free to travel. It is a cultural expectation in many countries to bring a spouse who is from another country home to meet family members. On our arrival, we visited my extended family in different parts of South Africa. These visits provided an opportunity for my ex-spouse and children to connect and learn about traditional practices and if so desired, immerse themselves in whatever appealed to them. As expected, my ex-spouse was curious to know more about the details of the traditional ceremony to include the slaughter of an animal, visiting my deceased parents at the graveyard, the early mornings of our ceremony, gum boot dance and about the preparation of home brewed ginger beer, the African beer made out of sorghum flour and about braai vleis. Another interest of his was to pronounce words in Xhosa and Zulu both of which were my deceased parents' languages, respectively. On the other hand, my daughters wanted to walk freely in Soweto visiting my cousins' homes. My brother who passed away years later was the host of our welcome party at the old family home. On the eve of the party, all the elders came to perform a customary practice to thank our ancestors for bringing me and my family home safe and to welcome their son-in-law. This was followed by the slaughtering of an animal, a sheep. As the preparations for the slaughter were underway and two animals had been brought in to the backyard, my daughters were obviously alarmed. They ran toward me saddened by what they were observing, the animals being dragged. They were disgusted to watch the merciless practice. They confronted me with questions. "How can you condone it, Mom, then eat that meat?" I tried to explain I grew up observing and respecting these practices. However, they just could not understand. The next morning, we were up early to make our homage visit to my parents' grave. It was a solemn event. My paternal aunt Agnes led prayers and salutations. We returned home to the smells of savory dishes which represented my intercultural family and community. Notably, through all this excitement, I watched with fascination, as my daughters enthusiastically responded to my aunt's request for help to set extra tables, as we were getting ready to have our feast. My daughters had seemingly forgotten everything about the previous day's gruesome slaughter of animals and their vehement objections. They were getting into the spirit of the moment.

Following the welcoming traditional ceremony, we began preparing for our first major trip to the Northern Transvaal to visit the animal kingdom at Kruger National Park. The timing of our visit was rather poor because animals were dying due to the country's worst drought. Luckily, a cousin had organized a braai and we had a great picnic at the park. On our next day, we visited several villages for the girls to witness ceremonial ritual dances by members of the Shangaan and Venda tribes, respectively. We met one of the village's superstars whose back-up singers were his five wives. Needless to say, my ex-husband was fascinated by this family of performers who had such an aspiration; to entertain in the US. They allowed us to video-tape their performances and begged us to pass it on to the US entertainment industry. They just would not take no for an answer.

Our next stop was a visit to Swaziland. I was very keen to take my family across the border to visit my aunt and my old schools. This trip took us to my former schools at Kwaluseni and St. Joseph's in Manzini. They were very impressed by Swaziland's mountainous countryside with lush vegetation interspersed with pine trees. Because of treacherous roads, it was risky to stop and admire the scenic views. Coming through the Oshoek border post, we were at Matsapa campus in Kwaluseni in two hours. Watching my children's reactions when they saw the warn-out buildings and poor conditions surrounding the schools, I wondered what they were thinking. I felt I should let them arrive at whatever conclusion they wanted because those were the buildings that sheltered me, gave me an education, love and made me who I became as their mother. For me, they represented fond, everlasting memories and inner peace. Our next destination was my aunt's place in Stegi which is south of Manzini on the way to old Lorenzo Marques, Mozambique. The last trip on our itinerary was to Cape Town to visit old school mates from the University of Zululand who had since moved to Cape Town and a few classmates I met in the US, who also lived in Cape Town.

We took this treacherous trip from Johannesburg driving through dry, deserted, lonely, boring roads of the Great Karoo on our way to Cape Town, praying that we did not run out of gas. I so much admired my ex-husband's daring, adventurous spirit in a foreign country, where, if he was stopped by police, he would not be able to speak in any of the local languages. Since he was on the assertive side and would stand his ground if confronted by police, I was constantly praying that nothing happened to us. At one point, he lost his focus while maneuvering through road blocks only to find himself on the wrong side of the road. We drew a sigh of relief when we finally entered the tunnel, heading toward Cape Town.

On arrival in Cape Town, we were able to navigate our way to the home of an old friend who, with his wife had offered to host us during our stay in Cape Town. Present at their home were other friends we had met in the United States who are residents of Cape Town. Though exhausted from the trip, we had a pleasant fellowship with our friends. The following day, our host took us on a tour of the of Cape Town's Black neighborhoods of Gugulethu, Zwelitsha, and Mdantsane. At the end of the tour, a nice get-together had been organized in the Western Cape with other friends. We were treated to a spicy stew called Potjie Kos which is cooked outside in a three-legged, cast-iron pot. The following day, we visited Table Mountain and the University of Cape Town which sits on a slope of the mountain. Our last excursion was to Cape Point, or to be precise, to the Cape of Good Hope where the Indian and Atlantic oceans meet. The most memorable time of that trip was taking photos of African penguins in their glory and being chased by baboons.

Much as we wanted to take the girls to Hout Bay to witness the so-called spectacular show with dolphins, we were running out of time in South Africa and had to head back to Johannesburg for our departure back to the United States. Two things that were omitted from our itinerary due to time and financial constraints were a ride on South Africa's luxurious Blue Train and a drive along South Africa's Garden route. It was ironic that though born and raised in South Africa, this was my first experience of Cape Town.

X

THE DEMISE OF A MARRIAGE

It is often said that marriage is 'work'. However, given the push and pull that one experiences in any relationship and certainly in a marriage, there is no definite formula to determine when, how and why things ultimately fall apart in a marriage? I have gone through this soul-searching process numerous times, wondering how some are able to make it, while others fail. I had to deal with these questions over and over because I was determined not to fail the second time. However, the inevitable happened. In fact, given all the horrible things that men and women do to each other when they no longer want to stay married, like hiring a hit man or throwing a spouse over a cliff, divorce is much better. Even the Catholic Church is considerate in that it grants an annulment in cases of domestic abuse. How do people who once loved each other to a point of getting married then find themselves hating each other enough to want their spouse eliminated? I have a hard time understanding such reasoning especially at the alarming numbers of murder mystery shows where a married partner suddenly disappears after the couple's vacation or honeymoon, or cases involving a cheating husband or a cheating wife. It is still admirable to know that there are people who still honor those sacred vows they made when they got married. It is also reasonable to attribute long-lasting marriages to sheer luck combined with a display of emotional intelligence by the individuals involved.

I have gone through self-reflection to understand how I perhaps might have indirectly sabotaged my marriages. Going back to my mid-thirties, I had an on-going struggle with wanting to be independent and at the same time, being dependent. I can trace this back to Mother who was my model. She epitomized hard-work and self-reliance. As a result, after my graduation from college, there was no hovering around doing nothing. I had to work. I worked for eight years. When I went to graduate school, my scholarship provided a monthly stipend, plus I worked part-time while my ex-spouse worked two jobs. In all honesty, he did not want me to work because we had a young child and I had to devote time to my school work. However, I had never wanted to be dependent on anyone but myself both financially and emotionally. The point is, being a strong-headed person, I could never visualize myself as a wife who tends to the home and children, waiting for my spouse to get home with dinner ready. There's nothing wrong in doing it for a spouse, I just was not cut-out for it. I can recall some of our nasty verbal exchanges when my ex-husband would finish off a sentence by saying, 'Yes, you do it because you are my wife'. Such utterances would set me on fire because they were laden with unpleasant insinuations. I would construe that he meant we were not equal in our marriage. To his insensitive statements, I would quickly respond saying, 'Oh! You thought you were marrying some stupid, passive African who is just too happy to be in the United States? Not this girl'. Not too long after, I would see sparks of flames bellowing through his eyes, a good time for both of us to step away from each other. One thing we had, was our friendship, the ability to laugh after a heated argument, to be playful with each other and to laugh at ourselves. He always teased me about my pronunciations of Massachusetts and Plymouth and the girls would join in. Luckily, our disagreements were short-lived. We genuinely loved and cared for each other. Despite my need for independence, I recognized that as a social being, I had to depend on a partner to fulfil those emotional and physical desires that I could not fulfil. So being married offered a safe place for our individual growth as well as that of our family. Moreover, we both needed a venting board when we came home from school or work. Marriage played a significant role in that manner, and that is why I will always respect the institution of marriage.

As things were settling well for me in my career, he was seriously considering joining another team which was based out of state, with promises of a lucrative package. This was the era of the information superhighway and the industry was at its height. In order to be on the cutting edge, it appeared one had to be willing to relocate to take advantage of better job offers. Such moves were fine for individuals without families. Besides, one had to factor in so many things such as a spouse's career and children's schooling. However, the offer he received from this company in Chicago was not in the best interests of our children who had moved four times. In addition, it most certainly was not in my interest coupled with the rigid requirements for one to move through to earning a tenured position. He proposed to try it for a year while I remained behind with promises of returning home bi-weekly but I knew right away, from a financial standpoint, it was not going to work. Since our efforts at problem-solving usually led to arguments, we went through numerous of those arguments over his decision. I struggled to support his decision. While I harbored a lot of my ignorance and stereotypes about certain cities in the United States, Chicago just happened to be a city I knew little about except when South Africa's mobster wannabes often equated their styles to Chicago's mobsters. I had no interest knowing about Chicago nor visiting it. Already we had gone through several moves because of his company, and had to deal with a lot of difficulties supporting our daughters to make smooth adjustments in their preteen years. Following those four relocations and dealing with their separations from friends who played such a vital role in their adolescent transitional stage, I had to be their advocate not to move again. Another move with our daughters to Chicago and me without a job in Chicago, was a completely unfeasible option. Part of me also resented the fact that he never had considerations for my career. If I were to agree to his deal I would have had to start all over again with job-searches and that grilling interview process which basically varied from one institution to another. Not only that. I would have had to know and buy into the politics of whichever school I ended up getting a job at. The latter becomes too taxing depending on who the individuals are that one has to please or appeal to, in order to move up the ladder of tenure and promotion.

My reasoning was driven by my personal experiences. I was born, raised and bred in the same house and community. This house is still standing. Though no longer occupied by its original family members, it is still occupied by my extended family. This is where I go when I say I am going home. I also understand that times are different. In order to make it in this society, one has to be prepared to make such moves. I also know the responsibility of parents and that is to be considerate of the other spouse's interests and career, as well as the developmental transitions that children go through. For him, I was willing to give him the compromise he wanted, by traveling back and forth between Chicago and New Jersey for a year and then determine the next move. Indeed, the trial period of commuting back home fortnightly worked for a while. It then changed to once a month. When he started experiencing difficulties in keeping up with the two visits per month, I braced myself for the worse. To me, it signaled an end to our compromise. As I thought more about what marriage is all about, I arrived at a conclusion that from my end, there were no benefits to be derived from this marriage whereas for him, they were still there. I not only viewed myself as a single parent, I handled all household responsibilities and the children's needs alone. For instance, for that duration of his absence, I had to rush home every day after a commute of ninety minutes to be on time to watch an athletic practice, a dance class or theatrical play that one of our daughters was in, then have dinner ready for them and monitor their homework period. I can clearly remember the few times he would come home. If he arrived on a Friday night, the agreement was that he would have to spend time with the girls by either taking them to their soccer practice or a dance recital and if none were taking place, find something to do with them. Quite often, he had an excuse. Of course, this meant, I had to do it. In all honesty, I empathized with him because that drive was totally ridiculous. Then there were times when I would watch him slouching on the coach, watching football or whatever game was on TV, then have the audacity of asking me, 'what are we having for dinner'. The feeling of resentment would completely cloud my thinking. At times I would be spiteful and cook a meal he did not want. When that happened, he liked to storm out of the house and return wearing a stone cold face, holding a KFC dinner box in one hand. Unable to hold ourselves back, the girls and I would break up in laughter. He would later confess, he was yearning for it but did not know how to express it, knowing I was strongly against it.

This picture of married life looked like a hoax to me. I felt, I could do it alone rather than depending on someone else. A wise person can see the writing on the wall when a partnership like a marriage is shifting its balance to favor one partner rather than the other one. I was not someone wearing blinders and did not want reality to hit home when it was too late. I felt I had given it my all. When he realized how serious I was with my decision, he solicited support from our friends but my patience had worn out. Unfortunately, the sweet memories we made together could not sustain our troubled union. He was a true friend, soul-mate, a husband, father and lover who genuinely wanted to hold on to a family he never had, as he would say. However, after fourteen years, we parted ways but remained good friends. We raised two beautiful daughters who admired him a lot. With a focus on my career, and this belief in myself, I worked hard to prove to myself and to whoever had doubts about me that I would gain tenure and a promotion. I like to give him credit for socializing me into the American culture. He often reminded me how he taught me how to drive on the right side of the road, brew and enjoy iced-tea instead of hot tea, differentiate soccer from football; pronounce schedule the American way, appreciate America's fond usage of certain words which I considered to be offensive. More importantly, he taught me the importance of being 'visible' at my children's schools and participating at parent-teacher conferences which he did without missing any. Again, this was due to his job's proximity to the school. Consequently, when I took over, I knew how to reach out to my children's teachers if I had concerns. He liked to constantly remind me, 'in this country, you do not share too much information. You are not in South Africa'. By the time I assumed the role of being a single-parent, I knew how to navigate the demands of my children's schooling and how to act as a disciplinarian, while establishing my career in academia. Tough as it was with so small a support system, I persevered to make it work.

There are many theoretical suppositions that are used to explain why marriages fail. Each time I come across those, I tend to reflect on my own childhood experiences to ascertain if there were any contributory factors on my side. However, considering that marriage failures cannot be attributed to one source, I would also explore childhood experiences of my ex-husbands that were shared with me, to determine if I could find answers. Of course, this tended to be a futile exercise because no one can claim to have had a perfect childhood. Also, there are individual who just want to view life only from their own perspective, no matter what. Unfortunately, in such situations, therein lies the ego-driven and narcissistic personalities. This is not to suggest he was egocentric. Not at all. It just took him time to realize there was no turning back from my side. Through our regular contacts, by the sixteenth year, he suggested we should perhaps consider reconciling and moving back to the South. Some of the ideas he presented never sounded practical to even suggest I leave my job to move out of state and rekindle our relationship. At the time, I was not even considering retirement. I could sense something was amiss. A year thereafter, he passed away. We were all devastated and for our closure, it was the right thing to do; attend his memorial service. I am forever grateful to God for the opportunity he gave us to heal from the pain we caused each other and the children by going through a divorce. We both matured and realized after years apart that we genuinely cared for each other but could not cure personal demons that were a huge barrier to simply embrace communication as a tool to problem-solving. The latter was a trigger for him. It made him feel and think I treat him as one of my clients or students.

Navigating life alone as a single parent of two teenagers, in a foreign land, far away from my village where I had a strong support system, was the biggest challenge. As a private person, I had few friends and even then, I preferred not to share much about how I was doing overall. My family back home kept close contact just to check on my well-being and the girls. One of the calls that used to get me really upset would be from my brother who is now deceased. He was fond of his brother-in-law. At times, it seemed he was not fully grasping that we were no longer together. Every call he made, his interest was to know how his brother in-law was doing. What about me? What about my girls? Granted, it was an unfair criticism on my part, but I expected some level of sensitivity from him as a brother. I also knew that given the distance; my family could not do much but demonstrate how they were dealing with their lose over the end of our marriage. Frankly, I do not know how I persevered. My plate was literally full. There are times when I cannot even remember how I did it. It was not only about attending to my daughters' needs but to the demands of my job as well.

XI

A MENTOR WHO RECOGNIZED MY POTENTIAL

There are so many people we meet on our life's journey. At times, we never fully understand how our roads cross each other. We might not even appreciate the impact they have on our lives nor get an opportunity to thank them until it is too late. This experience had happened to me before when, through a chance encounter, I met a White woman who did not know me from a bar of soap but would change the course of my life by paying for my college tuition to abate my dismissal from college. Little did I know that God had dropped another such meeting in my orbit and that was to meet my mentor at my new job after leaving my Florida teaching position. I was assigned to work with a full professor in my department. We were completely different. She was Caucasian American woman of Swedish descent, an only child, ten years my senior and a full professor in my department. From the time I joined the Department, I found her to be easy to engage with on a personal level. She was knowledgeable, heavily involved in academic activities within our discipline and scholarly active. Her work ethic and high energy was very attractive to me. She also showed much interest in guiding me along to make sure I was prepared for each class; that I was not encountering any problems with students and everything was running smoothly for me. Every day I was on campus, she would drop by my office with her usual greeting, 'Hey Jo, how's the going? How was class?', 'Feel free to call me at home' etc. She was authentic, friendly, sincere in everything she did or expressed. She made sure she shared resources with me each time she went to a national conference or meeting. She was popular with students of every race, ethnicity, gender and national background. They loved and respected her. On her office days, the entrance to her office would be packed with students. On such days, everyone in the department knew they could only reach her after her office hours. She wore this infectious smile which was extremely confusing because she could be having a disagreement with a colleague in a meeting but her demeanor would remain unchanged. The smile would be constantly there unabated. Out of curiosity, one day and this was years after we had been working together, I was experiencing some personal challenges with a colleague. I was in my office to regroup when she walked in, again, wearing her smile. She sat down and offered this suggestion, "Jo, you must not let people know they get under your skin." I justified my reaction by pointing out to the false claims which had been made by the other colleague. She continued, "But you must not let them know. Look at me, you see this smile? It has been my strongest weapon throughout my life because people can never know when I am upset. Even my husband finds it frustrating because he cannot read the exact meaning of my smile. When he starts arguing with me, I simply look at him, throw my smile, then watch his reaction as he gradually gets himself infuriated. When he's looking for something, he has no business asking me where it is, I put on my smile. By now he knows what to ask and not to ask. The same applies to students. When they attempt to manipulate me, I stand my grounds with a smile, and proceed on to remind them of our rules of engagement." In essence, I was impressed. I absorbed everything she said then thought to myself if I incorporate these ingredients into my life, I will be able to stay the course leading to tenure.

It was three years after I had joined the department that my mentor encouraged me to respond to an announcement, to participate in an educational delegation from the US with members of the delegation selected from the various parts of the country. The delegation was to visit Hong Kong and China for fourteen days as part of a cultural and educational exchange with various governmental entities in each country. Further, she advised me to seek partial financial support from the university. The university endorsed my request and my ex-husband who had moved to Chicago, willingly agreed to fly the kids to stay with him for the duration of my China trip. From this trip, I was able to discern some of the differences between my experiences in South Africa from those of my colleagues in the delegation who were not particularly used to the lifestyle of China at the time. I felt my adaptability was comparatively stronger in some instances compared to others. The stifling heat and poor air quality was intolerable to all of us. For example, the use of out-houses was quite common in China and I was familiar with it. Unfortunately, some members of my group found them to be beneath their expectations and deemed them deplorable. Yet to me, they were just meant for that purpose and nothing else. The absence of a McDonald restaurant nearby, unless one traveled to Beijing, was heart-wrenching to some. To be fair, the Chinese foods we ate there for the entire time of our stay from breakfast, lunch to dinner, were different in terms of taste from those sold and consumed in the US. Not only that, if one was expecting to have a chicken dish it never tasted like chicken but had an indistinct taste. Of course, that generated all kinds of speculations. Other than the misgivings of little things of comfort, there was so much to learn and appreciate from this trip. We visited silk factories and learned about the fascinating process that begins in a butterfly farm to the silk weaving factories to end up in exquisite garments. For the life of me, I would have never known had I not visited China. Another eye-opener was a visit to mental hospitals where lobotomy was still being practiced. A visit to Tiananmen Square brought tears to my eyes because it reminded me of South Africa's riot of June sixteenth 1976. We also took on the Great Wall of China during one of China's hot August days. To this day, I do not know how far I walked but it definitely could not have been more than four miles. Nevertheless, I was proud of my efforts. Outside the formalities of that visit which included formal meetings with government officials, personally, I was mostly fascinated by the co-navigation of each rider's right of way at major, unmarked intersections between bicycle riders and motorists, in the absence of traffic lights. The rhythmic coordination of the right of way between cyclists and motorists was absolutely a fascination of mine, like I could just stand there all day long watching and admiring their way of navigating the right of way. If you can take a moment to imagine a sea of bikers approaching an intersection from their respective four directions with motorists alongside them, then without any regulation, proceed on to enter the intersection while others waited their turn, was mind blowing to me. Given the huge number of bicycle riders compared to motorists, it seemed those who could afford cars were few. More importantly, it appeared that the encroachment of the west or modern world on the old culture was gradually approaching.

Indeed, looking at China today, particularly at cities we had visited, there has been major advancements in China in the last twenty-seven years. This trip to China became an impetus to my collaboration with my mentor on several projects involving international issues. Given my work experience in South Africa, she saw a great potential for me in exploring possibilities of establishing a faculty-student exchange with universities in South Africa, namely the university of the Western Cape and the University of Botswana. In addition, she saw this move as key to enhancing the department as it moved toward building a graduate program and attracting international students. Though both student-exchange possibilities fell-through as the political upheavals in South Africa continued to present safety concerns, our collaboration continued to expand. We worked on international conference presentations, increased the numbers of international students admitted to our program. As we continued working together on different projects, I got into the practice of reaching out to her frequently at home by phone for consultation purposes. As a morning person, I would call her in the morning hours between nine and ten a.m. and I would pick up on her grogginess, though she would never complain. However, she would suggest that I call her back after twelve p.m. Needless to say, I was oblivious to her sleeping patterns. She was not a morning person. She functioned well after twelve p.m. up to midnight. I was the opposite. I functioned well in the morning hours. I would also observe how she struggled when we go to a conference. When scheduled for early morning conference presentations, she would have a hard time handling it because she was a night person.

Inspired by my trip to China, I responded to an announcement for volunteers for an archeological dig in Israel. Though my initial interest in going to Israel was to explore possibilities of conducting a research study on the settlement of Ethiopian Jews, I decided going for a dig during my summer break would be a good experience. I remember landing at Ben Gurion Airport and being immediately pulled aside by young custom security woman for a search. Following the body search, I was interrogated at length about the purpose of my visit. What appeared to be raising eyebrows was the fact that I was a green card holder at the time, traveling on a South African passport. Luckily, I had documented proof of where I was going and the purpose of my visit. After an hour-long delay, I was finally let go. The dig was located outside Jerusalem at the Kibbutz Kfar Menachem. There were other volunteers there who came from different parts of the world and we all were provided accommodation within the kibbutz and were also expected to help out with house chores, when needed. The person in charge of the excavation site, Shmuel ensured that we were up early to start digging before it got intensely hot and humid. I can remember us having to be up by five a.m. and by sunrise, we had to be done because of the intensity of the sun. Our work was interspersed with sight-seeing trips to the Dead Sea, Jerusalem, Bethlehem, Tel Aviv and Masada National Park. We also got to see some of the most advanced irrigation schemes and visited homes for children. On my return to the United States and following the grilling immigration clearance I had to go through in order to be allowed into Israel, I was determined to apply for my US naturalization.

I returned from Israel with materials which I felt were going to help my mentor and I to pursue a research study of Ethiopian

Jews in Israel. Unfortunately, it turned out that that was not an opportune time as our department had entered a tumultuous phase with a power struggle brewing between those who had been in the department longer which included my mentor, I and others, with those who were newly hired. Besides, the growth from five to twelve faculty was a lot. It was difficult to agree on things. Also, what I discovered was that with academia, when new people join a department, they tended to think and act like they were the 'new broom that sweeps clean'. They had this tendency of quoting how things were done in their previous institution as if to say, 'let's do it the way we did it' wherever they came from. I still find that type of mentality to be frustrating and arrogant. The incoming group, perhaps due to their former work settings, they had different expectations. Somehow, they also appeared determined to introduce changes that were different from the way the department had been operating. At the same time, there appeared to also be an effort to ignore and undermine long-standing practices that were a tradition, earning the department stability, visibility and respect in the community. At least that was the way I viewed things. I valued the existing structure of the department and I was determined to remain loyal to my mentor. After all, she had been at that institution for twenty years, having served as an adjunct professor to eventually receive tenure and promotion to become a full professor. Had one warned me about nasty, political struggles in academia, I would have vehemently disputed such an analogy. However, it turned out to be true and ugly. Our department meetings were painful to attend and to sit through the shenanigans and unkind confrontations toward my mentor, was torturous. By that time, she had been appointed to serve as the chair of the department. Unfaced by all the drama, she would continue with her smile, respond to every question and remain cool and collected. In her assessment of the future prospects of the department, she felt I would be the second in line in the department. In light of that, she suggested that I should be heavily involved in the administrative matters of our department in order to learn the intricacies of running a department. This marked the shift in my roles from teaching to aiding administrative responsibilities. Because of my support of her, I came to realize that some members of the faculty were not fully endorsing my new role. Regardless, I was determined to remain loyal and supportive to my mentor. The extent to which the opposition group was prepared to destroy our reputation was astounding. On one of the days, I had my office hours, I encountered what I considered to be down and dirty behavior and claims made by one of the faculty members. This individual had walked into my office to request help. When she came in, I was engrossed in something else. I was eager to complete it lest I lost my trend of thinking. I turned to her and assured her, as soon as I was done I would come to her office. Indeed, as soon as I was done, I walked over to her office to assist with whatever she wanted done. I had been in that office for a few seconds, trying to comprehend what exactly she was asking of me. I was standing on the other side of her desk as she was talking, looking at and reading an email which I suspected it was an email I had sent out to faculty earlier about students' advisement when all of a sudden, she stood up from her chair, passed me and stormed out of her office leaving me behind, stunned. I walked behind, following her not knowing what she was running away from and what I had done. As I was following behind her, I asked myself, what just happened? It was the manner in which she stormed out of her office that bewildered me and anyone who was in the hallway watching this scene. It clearly looked like she was running away from something. Holding my head, I walked past the office she went to toward my office, totally shocked. I had hardly sat down for a few seconds when another member of faculty walked in to find out from me what had happened. While I could not decipher the exact comment she made as she mumbled under her breath, it sounded like she was aware of something about the other member' behavior. Shortly after her arrival in my office, campus police were at my door to take a statement. They took a statement from me to apparently weigh her statement against mine. Supposedly in her statement she claimed I was holding her hostage in her office by blocking the door. I was appalled. In no way could I have blocked her office door and to accomplish what?

I still remember that the incident happened in late April a week before that semester came to a close. I kept asking myself if this was a set-up, but for what? I had never experienced anything like it and more importantly, it was something I never envisaged happening at a university level. I was barred from discussing the situation with anyone since further investigations were on-going. She never reported for classes or her office hours after that day. In fact, that was to be the last day that faculty member was on campus. I kept on playing and replaying that day's event to comprehend what actually led to it but each time, I came up empty. For my protection, I kept a copy of the statement I had submitted to campus police and a copy of the findings of campus security, which I still have to this day. I have never stopped wondering what was behind that situation. I always revisit her mood when she first came to my office to ask for help and from her demeanor, she was her usual self, giggling. How could I have done what she claimed given her physical stature. She could have easily done any number of things to defend herself, if she had wanted to. She could have pushed me aside and dragged me out of her office to the hall way. Afterall, I stood at five foot four inches weighing under one hundred and thirty pounds. She was five foot seven and had a weight of approximately one hundred and sixty pounds. In no way could I have put my hands on her. I am not a violent, aggressive or crazy person. In fact, this was part of the campus police findings that under no circumstances could I have physically threatened her. I tortured myself for many years trying to understand what was behind her unpredictable behavior, and how I could have contributed to it. Was the faculty member who came to my office and mumbled something aware of something amiss about her? To date, I still do not know. All I know is that the angel that watched over me from my early childhood years was beside me that day and continues to stay there still.

I began to think of my first experience at that private university in Florida and the behavior of the two faculty members who would stand by my classroom door to eavesdrop on my delivery of lectures assumably because I had a 'strange accent' or perhaps because students had complained to them but I was never made aware of it? Were all these experiences I had been subjected to typically indicative of academia? Perhaps not. Given that the common denominator was the presence of a Black woman and a foreigner in the middle of all these minutiae, could that possibly explain these phenomena? Was it a lack of tolerance or, perhaps slightly better, acceptance of someone different?

These are tough questions that raise so many uncomfortable issues. However, I am of the opinion that not all problems of this nature could be only analyzed and understood within the scope of race. Sometimes it can be attributed to layers of arrogance, entitlement and desperation. Regardless, it is how they are handled, that makes the difference.

Another academic year resumed that August, and things continued to be chaotic. However, we were able to prevail – to end the year without major incidents. The winter holidays gave us time to reflect and regroup. My mentor had indicated to me that she and her husband were going to be traveling to one of the Caribbean islands where they were looking at a retirement property. When classes resumed after that winter break, my mentor did not show up that first day, it was unusual for her to be absent. Later that day, I received a call from my mentor stating she suddenly took ill over the winter break and had reached out to the office of human resources to request time off. She also indicated she reached out to her students to make sure her absence was not interfering with their learning. She had provided them with out of class assignments. Even when I talked to her over the phone, I could tell she was devastated by being away from the classroom and her students. Teaching was her passion and the classroom was where her heart was. Time went by with the hope that she was coming back. By the second month of her absence she called again to inform me her doctor was recommending her to not return. Further, she stated she was going to reach out to the provost to recommend that I run the department until her return. I knew I could handle the task but I was not sure how this would be received by the rest of faculty given that some were not thrilled with me assuming the position of chair even on a temporary basis. They saw themselves as the next in line. Indeed, the following week, I received an official letter of appointment from the provost affirming that I would be serving on an interim basis until her return. I continued to consult with her by visiting her at home. Every time she would throw me off with her smile as if her condition was not that serious and I respected her way of dealing with it. I was fortunate to have another colleague who graciously stepped up to help me. We worked together well and completely ignored all criticisms that we heard being thrown at us. It was tough, but we were determined to make her proud of our efforts to do her job as she would have done it.

Her condition began to deteriorate. She was admitted to hospital and I continued to visit her in hospital. I also had hopes that she would let me know what her diagnosis was but each time, I would get that smile, 'Oh Jo I don't know where to start'. Again, out of respect, I would not pursue the discussion. Though I had no medical background at all, however, because of the change in her demeanor and appearance, I deduced that whatever it was, she was not getting any better. We talked at length about the work she wanted me to complete which was in her office and saved on her computer. She gave me thorough briefings on how to prioritize and schedule classes for faculty, manage my time to make sure I was ahead of the game, emphasizing to me that the job was twenty-four seven not an eight or nine to five. Throughout this time, she reaffirmed my abilities to do the job, 'Jo, you can do it. I have confidence in you'. She made me really proud to know just how much confidence she had in me. I was also determined not to fail her, but to ensure that when she returned back to assume her duties, she would not be disappointed. Unfortunately, this was not to be. A week before Thanksgiving, I received a call with a few details from her husband to meet him at the hospital. My brain automatically went back to my own personal experience when I made my last visit to Mother at the hospital. I started asking God, why me? Should I go through this again? Was she going to make it? I braced myself and met her husband in the hallway that led to her ward. I could not read his face as he approached me. In a somber voice, looking away from me, he proceeded to tell me that the previous night the doctor's had told him they could not do anything else for his wife. He then advised me to remain calm and be aware she was in no state to talk. Right there, I panicked but silently prayed for strength to see her and not fall apart. While standing outside her ward, a hospital chaplain came out of the ward and the nurse ushered us in. I seemed to recall the nurse saying, "Talk to her, she will be able to hear but not respond." I stood there, helpless and watched her husband sobbing quietly. He pulled himself up and we went in. Borrowing from my culture, I suggested to him we should say a prayer. Standing at the foot of her bed, we started praying. We could not stop our emotions, the sadness that was suddenly engulfing us with tears trickling down our faces as we watched her life slowly ebbing away. I was in so much pain but could not even imagine the pain that her husband was going through. She meant so much to him. For me, she was not only a dear friend, colleague, a mentor; she was like a sister. I thought about the burden I had to carry to perform at her level. I remember her common comment when she would say to me, 'Jo it is lonely up here. When everyone is pointing a finger at you for something that went wrong and they choose not to take responsibility for it, you have to take it and not complain, to keep the peace even when you know you are not at fault'. It seemed now it was my turn to experience the challenges of administrative responsibilities. I thought to myself, now I have to deal with that loneliness without her to advise, guide or intervene. Already, I had made a few observations of disgruntled individuals in the department. I was not oblivious to the fact that I was a foreigner, a Black woman with an accent and that at times, was used as an excuse to be rude, to undermine me and frankly to suggest I was not capable of running the department. I made a promise to my mentor that nothing was going to deter me from doing what needed to be done. Thankfully, another colleague stepped in to assist me and we were able to work together pulling together some of the loose ends. In addition, we organized a dignified memorial service for our departed colleague.

The emptiness that one feels at the top did not hit me until I was faced with another crisis and did not know who to turn to. I needed a confidant. I finally reached out to someone outside the department who was gracious enough to meet with me on a regular basis, giving me space to vent. Those meetings were helpful and allowed me to convince myself that I could do it, and shut out the noise. Soon thereafter, I was asked to serve the rest of my mentor's term as chair of the department. I was also notified that at the end of her term which was in two years, faculty had to have elections to choose another chair.

Sometimes, there are certain devious behaviors that one does not expect to see at the higher levels of education. For me this has a lot to do with high expectations for people at higher academic ranks to conduct themselves with high levels of integrity. The majority of my colleagues were professionals and maintained high standards of ethical behavior toward each other. However, when the discussions about elections for a new chairperson resumed, it got too complicated. For one, I knew I was done and had no interest to seek nor accept a second term. Besides, I did not want my appointment to continue to be a source of polarization in the department. To my surprise, a lot of things that were going on behind the scenes were beginning to appear on my radar. I received information that the colleague who worked closely with me was going around pressuring someone who was not interested to run, to put in her name. In the meantime, another individual was calling me at home to encourage me to put in my name. His rationale was to thwart the chances of winning for the other person. Also, he was of the opinion that it was important for me to continue in that position so as to ensure that the stability of the department was maintained. This individual was someone I truly respected for his intelligence and commonsense. When I thought about the latter, I immediately decided to run for a second term. I was also troubled to think there were individuals who were still not in favor of my interim appointment running the department.

It has been my practice to never run to judgement by accusing people who might not be in agreement with and of a different race and attribute it to racism. Though it had occurred in my mind about this person, I quickly dismissed it. I reasoned; we were just one of those departments that got caught up in a lot of politics which led to changes in our administrative structure. As a result, people were not happy about it. My position was firm and that position was to maintain stability and to ensure that the passing of our chairperson did not affect students' academic progress. Winning the second election was to me, a symbolic win for my mentor. I felt their full endorsement, except for one person, was a validation and a testament of the hard work I had put in to keep the department afloat.

XII

A TEST OF MY FORTITUDE

The upcoming four years of chairing a department were going to be a test of my character. I felt encouraged and empowered by the votes I had received from faculty, to serve with confidence. Of importance was the responsibility of carrying forth some of the initiatives of my predecessor. This was also a critical time to work toward the reaffirmation of the program's accreditation status. There were three faculty members with the expertise I needed to see that process move forward. We had started with our organization plan when, to everyone's surprise we received word that a new candidate was being interviewed by the administration. Such a process was unheard of. Departments made such decisions themselves. However, it turned out that the candidate who was being interviewed had been recommended to the administration by one member of our faculty because of her expertise in program accreditation. This was done without consultation with me and the rest of faculty.

Years thereafter, it was revealed to me that a quid pro quo might have been at the heart of that arrangement. Indeed, this individual joined our department and she turned out to be a resourceful person. However, her presence kept many of us on edge because there was no clarity to the reason behind her hiring. Faculty took on their respective responsibilities seriously without additional assistance from her. At one point I was able to retain a consultant to assist in the review of a self-study before it was submitted. By the end of that year, she appeared disillusioned, and resigned. With the support of faculty, I was able to carry on the functions and responsibilities of my role. Toward the end of my tenure, and with the then president's efforts to replace department chairs with executive directors, a search committee began looking for someone to take over as the executive director. The individual who was finally selected turned out to be one of the discipline's prolific writers whose textbooks are used nation-wide. Personally, I had used his books since I started teaching. I highly respected him. I was however soon to find out he was after my blood. I can recall his first visit to campus for a meeting with faculty. We had gone to lunch. After lunch, I offered him a ride to campus. He asked me a few questions then wanted to know, who of us was the faculty member from Africa. I was seriously taken aback. I responded, 'Oh! That's me.' My response seemed to have taken him by surprise or was so unexpected that I did not get a follow up word thereafter.

His tenure started off fairly well with all of us demonstrating our support. I also took it upon myself to apprise him from the administrative angle, on how the process worked. I made myself available to him as much as I could, but it turned out he would not seek any directions from me. I was fine with his approach because he was a seasoned teacher and an administrator from his previous positions. There was a part of me though that wondered if the administrator of the college might have said unfavorable things to him about me. Though I used to have a good working relationship with the administrator of the college, he had tried to undermine my intelligence to protect a director of another unit. I had gone to his office for something else. As I was about to leave,

153

he asked me if I would be willing to help him resolve a situation facing another director in his college. Reportedly, the director, a White male and a Black female employee on his staff were not getting along too well. The college administrator also a White male and thought I could help by swapping my department's secretary for the Black female employee. As I tried to explore the nature of their problem, it turned out to be insubordination. I questioned the administrator of my college about how he thought I would be able to handle someone who would be difficult to work with. His suggestion was to 'doc' her. He emphasized, 'just document and send the report to me'. I could not believe he was that blatant. By this time, I am seething with anger. Where is our integrity in such a practice? Using me to do this dirty work just did not appeal to me. At that moment, I felt insulted and reacted instantly. I stood up and told him I was not about to do it, and that I would be prepared to be fired rather than to take on that person. I went on to explain to him that the fact that we were both Black females did not necessarily mean we were going to work well together. Further, I made it clear to him that as administrators, we were all expected to know how to work with our members of staff rather than resort to such shenanigans. He seemed stunned by my reaction. However, for me, it had a lot to do with feeling disrespected and used. As I left that office, I wondered to myself if he could have tried that foolish trick on someone else. Our exchange was unpleasant and unfortunate. It fractured our working relationship to the point that by the time the new executive director started his tenure, I had lost faith in the administrator of the college. Hence, I was taken aback when the onboarding executive director asked a question about an African faculty member.

Now as a faculty member and no longer an administrator, I felt a lot of weight was off my shoulders. My focus now was on my teaching responsibilities. At the same time, I was feeling uneasy with the question the new director had asked, presumably not knowing I was the African he was asking about. Also, some of the spiteful comments he would make about the prior administration during department meetings were ill-informed and hurtful. Obviously, there were philosophical differences in our style of leadership and our interpretation of the profession's academic standards and policies. However, I began to realize he was completely out of line and outdated in his approach to administering an accredited program. I began doing my own research about him and his writings related to the profession, and consulted with colleagues in other schools. Not everyone was willing to be forthright about what they knew of him as an administrator or a teacher. Almost everyone would latch onto his caliber as a prolific writer and scholar at which, undoubtedly, he was outstanding, nationally and internationally. In my searches I came across only one negative review posted by a student on a website basically stating he did not belong in the classroom. Personally, I had a similar review a while back from a disgruntled student. So, I did not find this too informative. I was finally able to read an article he had written which I found disturbing primarily because it was advocating for an overhaul of the educational curriculum content of the profession. The article was shocking to me. It also shed a lot of light for me in terms of what he was attempting to do with the program. I reasoned, I was already too controversial in many ways and could not take the administrator of the college into my confidence. I just stood back and watched since no one else was questioning anything he was doing. To his credit, he was coaching students in writing articles

155

for publications which students found profoundly gratifying; to read their own published articles. Meanwhile, I continued to feel harassed, intimidated and humiliated. However, I took it all in stride. In my previous life, I had dealt with ignorant, unpolished and obnoxious White male Afrikaners. This was not new to me at all. I surmised, he was fighting his own demons and felt the responsibility to clean a slate that just so happened to be occupied by an African woman. To me, that was his problem, not mine. The shocking and disappointing part though was that no one ever came to my defense. In all the years I had labored to keep the department afloat, given all the transitions we went through, while teaching and managing a satellite program that eventually had to close due to low enrollments, I never got the time to publish. In one of the department meetings we had, the new executive director circulated a chart he had developed with every faculty's name on it, to include individuals who had recently joined the department. Basically, the chart was to illustrate how many articles each faculty member had published the previous year. Beyond the publications, there were no other categories listed indicative of scholarship such as creative works, program reviews, conference presentations, or any criteria to depict administrative responsibilities. As he passed copies of this chart around the table, he looked at me. I took a glance at the copy in front of me. Next to my name was a zero, but for everyone else, it was one or two publications. I pushed the paper to the middle of the table, and looked at him as to ask for the meaning of this paper. He went on to talk about the need for publications and how he planned to enforce it. As a way of breaking through the tension that was engulfing the room, a colleague questioned the absence of conference presentations and other types of performances that were deemed to constitute scholarship. She then cited my situation and the administrative responsibilities I had done. Toward the end of this meeting which was nothing else but a display of ignorance, arrogance, humiliation and utter stupidity for any administrator to use as a form of mentoring and/or supporting his subordinates, the executive director pulled copies of a recent publication of his to distribute around the table and asked us to read it. Lastly, offered to help anyone with interest in publishing. I again pushed my copy to the middle of the table, stood up and left.

For the next few weeks, I felt he was earnestly creating an uncomfortable work-place environment for me. The fall semester was coming to a close. I felt the situation getting worse and unpredictable. Since I taught on Saturdays and the last Saturday of classes I knew students would not show up for class. I debated if I should go to class or not but decided to go. The conflict was due to students' past patterns of not showing up for class on the last day of class that fell on a Saturday. However, with what I perceived to be a change in my relationship with my supervisor, I felt I had to play it safe and go to campus. When I arrived on campus, I went to my classroom. A colleague who was also teaching that Saturday came by to my classroom to ask me if I had seen our boss walking around the building. I told her I had not seen him. She asked me if I thought he was snooping around. I told her, I had no knowledge of it but I was alarmed by the thought and decided that I would be watchful. Soon after she had left my classroom, I became agitated and kept my gaze on the classroom door which had a glass window in the middle whereby if inside the classroom, one could easily see a figure outside, should they pass the classroom door. Indeed, I saw a figure walk hurriedly past the classroom I was in. By the way, no student had showed up for class. I immediately dashed out of the classroom and headed toward the direction he was going. I did not see him. Since I was on the third floor, I could look down the railings to view anyone walking around on the lower floors. Indeed, there he was walking toward the stairway to leave the building. Shocking is not the word to describe how I felt. I sat in that empty classroom until the end of the class session. Luckily, I had brought student papers to read and grade. I felt I could not focus on my grading as I was growing anxious.

On my way home, I revisited the conversation I had with the administrator of the college which was about the Black female worker he wanted transferred to our department and the expectation that I had to watch her every move and document every activity that constituted a violation of her employment conditions. As I processed that conversation, I began to wonder if the same suggestion was being applied to me in terms of being watched with all of my activities documented. I could not wait for that fall semester to come to an end so I could have a winter break to re-coup my sense of being, meditate and gain some insight into the situation that was at play in my department where I had suddenly found myself at odds with the head of the department. On our return that spring semester, I received a request from him for a meeting which I attended. At the meeting which was attended by others who had been invited, he emphasized the importance of publication as one of the criteria for promotion. I decided I was going to listen attentively and accord him the respect as my supervisor. Having worked at that institution for years, I fully understood how important publication had become. I also knew about the unfairness of the process which outwardly appeared to be the demand for sound scholarship yet, such standards were applied selectively and differentially. I was also sensitive to the fact that as an accomplished scholar, he was new to the institution and was trying to make an impression by motivating everyone to engage in scholarship for the betterment of the department and the university. However, it was also true that he might not have known the extent to which that department had, over the years struggled to stay afloat due to limited resources to hire more faculty and support staff. In addition, there were other historical dynamics that were at play which had made the department very unpopular in the eyes of the head of the university. As a result, there were several individuals who opted for voluntary resignations. The department suffered the aftermaths of those historical situations to the extent that some of the remaining faculty members felt they were unfairly being penalized. For example, there was a constant push and pull that was experienced because of the administration's demand to increase enrollments at the expense of delivering a quality education and knowing fully well that the resignations had significantly reduced our faculty size.

It is unclear what the new administrator had been told because prior to his appointment, the previous chair and faculty had found themselves in awkward positions of having to control enrollments in order to maintain the educational standards and policies of the accrediting body. However, some of those policies were not popular with the administration. In particular, the accrediting body required specific limits on class size for certain course in order to maintain their mandate on teacher to student ratio. This situation created tough choices for the department. These choices meant going against the administration's requirements of increasing class sizes in favor of the accreditation guidelines of the program. Understandably so because the latter was our bread and butter yet at the same time, the violation of accreditation standards was equally risky. Therefore, faced with these overall prevailing conditions, the priority during my tenure as chair of the department was largely focused on risk management than on publication. Unfortunately, my attempt at explaining my circumstances to the new program administrator which had led to lack of publication for all those years I served as a 'crisis' chair of the program, fell on deaf ears.

Despite what he knew and/or did not know, the manner in which he handled that situation was somewhat harsh and it seemed much more personal than professional. This observation was also made by others who sat in on the meeting and had witnessed his interactions with me. They were able to diffuse the situation by apprising him about the culture of the university community which primarily had an emphasis on respect and sensitivity toward others, regardless of their background. In addition, they highlighted how things were done at this university. Primarily, they informed him about how the university's process was conducted to evaluate tenured faculty with promotion. In essence it meant that faculty in those ranks were to be evaluated by members of their peer group not by an administrator of his rank. Seemingly, no one had ever took the time to enlighten him about this process. This part of the meeting signaled the abrupt end of that meeting. Watching this full balloon slowly losing air to a point of depletion, was sad. I left that meeting feeling sad. That academic year ended in a dramatic way for me but that was to be just the beginning of the end.

In July of that year while we were all on summer break, an email was sent out to those of us who were affiliated with my department announcing the departure of the administrator of our department who only had completed one year of his tenure. Those of us who had experienced his wrath, consulted with each other to find more details about his departure. Meanwhile, the administrator of the college had contacted me to request that we meet. I consulted with other colleagues for suggestions. Out of their concerns for the department, they asked me to honor his request. Indeed, we met and were able to shelve our differences and all that had happened between us. Without spelling out details which, based on what I had heard through the grape vine was embarrassing and a sign of desperation, I did not want to know. I had already experienced the worst treatment from him, and that was enough. In his request for a meeting, he simply indicated to me that our former boss had left. He then asked me to step in on an interim basis because I had done this job before, and reassured me that he had confidence in my abilities. He also emphasized that I had to make it my priority when the semester began to put up a job announcement for a replacement for the upcoming year. We had a good meeting which turned out to be a bittersweet resolution to our old wounds. I offered to start looking at registration numbers to ensure that every course was covered. According to enrollment numbers, the incoming group of students was unprecedently the largest for the program. Therein lay the problem. It appeared that a number of applications that had been received during the summer were automatically dumped into the system under accepted. In consultation with the administrator of the college legal requirements meant I had to deal with that huge incoming class. Decisions could not be reversed. Now I had to open several sections for each course and scramble to find instructors. That summer turned out to be an unusually busy summer.

As I braced for the beginning of a new academic year, I was

anxious, not sure how returning students were going to deal with another administrative change.

At the beginning of that semester, students were visibly surprised. While some were disappointed to learn about our former administrator's departures, others were looking for some form of stability and a reassurance that they would graduate. My colleagues and I worked judiciously to support our students, make adjustments and focus on their education, while putting much effort into recruitment strategies for a new executive director. Though the climate in our work environment had significantly improved, there were major challenges with a number of students who had been wrongly assigned to courses and as a result, they were out of sequence in their course assignments. This meant their anticipated graduation dates would be affected. The extent to which program policies and standards had been violated was excessive. I spent time attempting to clean the mess out, while dealing with disgruntled students who felt this was demonstrable incompetence on the part of our program. Precisely how else were they supposed to explain it? While in some cases, there had been lots of oversight and failures to some degree, the errors were reflective of someone who either did not have a structure or of someone who was trying to create a new system or a new program and new curriculum. In the middle of that academic year, a resignation was announced by the administrator of the college. At this point, I became curious to know what was behind his resignation, and if it was related to the departure of our department boss. I became incessantly desperate to recruit a permanent executive director for the coming year so I could step down and return to teaching. There was too much drama going on which was accompanied by a dark cloud hovering around the department. I just could not put a finger on what was happening behind the scenes. All I knew was that I needed some semblance of order, peace of mind and normalcy. Therefore, I needed to be out of that position.

Finally, we interviewed and hired a Black male as the new department administrator. While I thought this was going to be the beginning of a positive new chapter, it was a disaster. It turned out to be one of my most disappointing performances and the worse period of my work experiences in higher education. I attributed it to my sense of desperation to find someone to replace the previous administrator. It was an effort on my part too to avoid serving another year as an interim director. One year of cleaning up his mess was enough for me. Trying to detail the backward draconian leadership that we were all subjected to, and the loss of professionalism that undermined ethical standards, would revive old wounds but also give credence to behaviors that are beyond the scope of my interests. There are numerous adjectives I could pick to describe the person and the situations he created. Again, to do so, would dignify his brief moments of glory. He was there for one year and gone that summer. The take away from these experiences under male leadership regardless of race, was extraordinary.

As someone who regularly practices self-reflection, I have tried to find a piece of me that contributed to the unhealthy working climate I was subjected to. While I have been unable to find answers, there is a part of me that acts in defense wherever I sense, I am being unfairly treated. I would also assume other people are like that anyway. Possibly that happened with both males. Also, because of my thirty years of experiences living under a racist and oppressive regime in South Africa, I do not use such terms as racist, discrimination and White privilege, loosely. I know the extent to which these practices can be severely damaging to people. Hence, it has never been my practice to call attention to myself by accusing others of practicing racism, or discrimination against me unless there is clear evidence of their intention to do so. But given the situations that I experienced, I often wonder if the individuals in question were unknowingly using either one of these practices to get what they wanted and solidify their positions. Afterall, they were dealing with an African woman who, perhaps in their thinking, ought to have been just too obliged to do what their boss wanted. I doubt I will ever understand.

This was not the end of my headaches. The next person to come to this position was an expert of his craft. What I experienced and learned from this individual, a Black administrator was that when people are desperate to get a job that allows them to wield power over others, they will employ cut-throat practices to get ahead. Quite often Black people talk about being invisible to White people. Yet they do the same to other Black people who are foreigners. Sadly, I experienced it from this individual. I became invisible to a Black person whose skin color was just like mine. Of the number of applications, we had reviewed, this was someone whose resume and interview ranked higher compared to others. After he was tapped for the position, he went through a period of rigmarole deciding where to go because, he 'had other offers'. Not wanting to lose him to those other universities that he claimed were interested, I spent time and earnest phone calls during my personal time to answer all questions he had about the position. When he finally decided to come to us, the tables were turned against me. One hears about this assumption that Black

164

people do not and will not discriminate against other Black people. It is a fallacy to believe so. I have since witnessed disturbing incidents whereby I have either been perceived as an enemy by those who look like me or as someone who thinks they know everything. I like to see people succeed and when I know how things are done and how to avoid unnecessary pitfalls, I tend to be too keen to help or advise. I also forget that some people do not take kindly to advice. One in particular, was a person I had gone to bat for during hiring. Later on, this person replaced the last administrator of the program who had left. As time went on, I found myself extremely frustrated with the manner in which she handled situations that were more associated with her position as someone in charge. Perhaps since I had held that position before, and happened to be the one who would ask a lot of questions to pass on the answers to students who were filling my email box with questions, that was a source of annoyance. Timely response to critical questions was lacking, the information that was communicated to faculty would sometimes be shallow, untimely with curt responses to critical question as if she was being unnecessarily bothered. There were times when I felt this person was turned off or annoyed at the questions which to me were part and parcel of the position. My level of frustration was characterized as anger, as in the stereotypical notion of an angry Black woman. I surmised from that statement that the aim was to divert attention from the real situations that I was addressing.

Given all the politics at my work-place and the lessons-learned from my administrative roles, the classroom had always been my forte. I derived much energy and gratification from my students in the classroom. Through teaching, I also became a student and a learner. I learned that being in America and raised in an

165

English-speaking country with free and compulsory education did not necessarily mean everyone would come out of that educational system as a liberally educated person particularly as it related to graduate expectations and performances. Similar to my native country, not everyone belonged to graduate school. Higher education had become such a big business that while some could make it, others struggled with the material and it became the professor's responsibilities and sometimes failure to try to help them because they lacked the basic skills to master content at graduate levels. I continue to challenge students to excel in whatever they do, more importantly I do this for Black students because others did it for me. I also understand that my approach has not been well received by some. However, whenever I get a chance to explain why I am this tough on them, I use myself as an example to impress upon them that when one is of a certain shade, one has to always aim high and be ahead of the game because the outside world has high expectations for us.

XIII

OPULENCE IN THE MIDST OF DESTITUTION

Though I have made frequent visits back and forth to South Africa for significant family events, the one I made in 2019 with my daughter and sister who is based in Toronto, became one that truly opened my eyes to the depth of the country's economic and social decay. We purposely checked into a hotel in the metropolitan area of Johannesburg for several reasons. Primarily, we needed access to internet services, accessibility to public transportation, access to uninterrupted telephone services and fresh produce were key factors. Our decision to stay in the suburbs as opposed to staying in Soweto was the most difficult one because unbeknownst to many, it is much safer to stay in Soweto than to stay in the suburbs. The suburbs are where the wealthy people live. Besides, if you break into a house in Soweto or rob someone, the community will come for you. There is still that spirit of Ubuntu in Soweto that one does not find in the suburbs. People self-isolate in the suburbs and there is little interest in wanting to know one's neighbors.

During this recent visit, I was finally able to make a definite decision that returning to South Africa for retirement would be the dumbest thing I could do to myself and my family. I made this decision not out of self-preservation but out of a consideration for my children and their families. Whereas I left my native community alone to find a better place for the children I would be raising, I have to be considerate of their own welfare and the care of their loved ones by not subjecting them to unnecessary conflicts of choosing if they should join me in South Africa or remain in a country that has been home to them for more than forty years. I am not Jesus the Messiah to right all the wrongs of this world, in particular, of South Africa. I bleed inside because there are millions of people who have waited for fifty years for justice to be delivered for them by Nelson Mandela's African National Congress. Instead, they have watched their promised land being carved up for foreign governments, friends and politicians' families. Where is justice? Some of them have since died waiting. There are those who have literally been left behind since the upheavals of the 1970s and 1980s. The prospect of ever witnessing any changes to bring opportunities for them have slipped away. Dare I say, though surprised by the current state of South Africa, I am constantly reminded of rumors we used to hear in the late 1960s about ANC leaders who were not necessarily fighting for our freedom from apartheid's bondage but living abroad in lavish styles, with summer houses in the Alps of Switzerland. Needless to say, we could only relate to the Alps of Switzerland by paging and reading through the picturesque National Geography magazine. To us, those attractive lifestyles were so far removed from our simple existence. However, looking at it now and weighing on those rumors and scenarios with the ANC's recent notorieties, I am beginning to see and understand the hypocrisy, the lack of a system of checks and balances and overall incompetence. Amongst so many other areas of deterioration in the country is the squalor of many parts of Johannesburg. The big question to many people in South

Africans is, how on earth did South African airline that was one of the top world ranked airlines drop to number forty-six in 2019.

The most unsettling sight for me to see when I visit my beloved country are the faces that are filled with the desperation and hunger everywhere I go. I see the same faces on visits with family members who count the years since the last time they had a job, a pay check or a meal. The thought that there is absolutely nothing I can do about it, is the most torturous feeling to bear. These are not lazy people, nor people who were ever accustomed to handouts because South Africa had none during the apartheid era. Black people lived for work and they enjoyed it. For the years I worked as a social worker in Soweto the only petty cash we kept as social workers was to give clients' money for a monthly train or bus fare to go and look for jobs. Appeasing people with government grants came with the advent of the ANC. Unfortunately for the recipients, they did not know the long-term effects of the government dole. It was ironic that when the United States was getting away from these public assistance programs, South Africa was embarking on them full force. When I heard about these public assistance programs in South Africa, I became curious to know their purpose. Were they designed to appease and buy the populace's loyalty to the ANC as an established voting block? Despite the ruling government's failures to deliver for the people, they remain popular. A longtime colleague asked me one time during a visit to South Africa to describe what I thought of government assistance programs. I suggested to her to read Cloward and Piven's 1971 book on, *Regulating the Poor*, and determine the book's relevance or irrelevance to South Africa's situation.

Over the past fifteen years, I have had family members admitted to one of the best training hospitals in South Africa, Baragwanath Hospital only to end up with death certificates due to the poor standard of care. Overall, the state of health care is in disarray. Food prices are ridiculously high. There are rolling-blackouts of electricity which means one has to cook and take a shower at certain times. I have found myself in serious debt each time I return back from my trips to visit family because I am a giving person. I listen to family members' sad stories of not being able to find jobs. Some would give accounts of family members who are able to assist but choose not to. The fiber that used to bind family members has been destroyed as people fight for their own survival. Then there are those who supposedly make excuses for not extending job opportunities to family members for fear of violating their employers' nepotism policies. The day I was told about the latter excuse, I realized just how unethical and greedy people had become. The world becomes a better place for everyone when we can all share in the abundance that has been given to us.

The challenges facing my community and South Africa as a whole are compounded by the relentlessness flow of immigrants and refugees from many parts of Africa and other countries. It was disheartening to observe that indeed, the rest of Africa has descended on South Africa. The sight of adults, children, women and men standing or sitting and begging on street corners and traffic intersections, some disabled and unkempt, in major suburban areas of the city, is something that South Africans are not accustomed to. This is due to the fact that there were national agencies for the blind, the disabled and visually impaired and for the mental ill which provided services to meet the needs of every vulnerable group, to include providing employment opportunities under sheltered employment. So, watching these groups taking to streets to beg on regular basis, was rather disconcerting to me. One time, I took this concern to someone, a local South African professional. She indicated that these people came to South Africa specifically in pursuit of the generous welfare programs. As a result, the general perception of South Africans is that many Africans are descending on South Africa because of the open borders, liberal human rights provisions, and generous welfare programs. This type of an analogy speaks volumes to the complexity of South Africa's problems, amidst blatant corruption, incompetence in leadership. It would seem to me that a country with a painful legacy such as South Africa would make it a priority to have strong infrastructures that protect the interests of its own citizens first, before extending their generosity to others.

Sadly, I have heard so many frustrated South Africans who are in the country and outside echoing the same sentiment, that their lives and the lives of loved ones were by far better off during the apartheid regime than they are now.

Personally, I have reflected on those sentiments myself as I reminisce about the Soweto of the past that nurtured me to be who I became. The most trying times produced some of the most talented, outstanding and accomplished professionals, musicians, writers, and technicians of our times. Beyond the failures of this government, the question to ask is what has led to this discrepancy between today's generations and those of past years? Families have tried to carry on the traditional practices of raising children and abiding by their customary practices. In addition, the country's educational system plays a significant role in the process of socialization. It will be interesting to know how it has fared since the riots of 1976, given that those riots were caused by the poor quality of education that was embedded in the educational system for Black South Africans. Based on my readings, the constant curriculum changes, poor pay for teachers and working conditions have led to sporadic strikes and a piecemeal structure in public education. However, for those who can afford it private schools that follow an international curriculum are available but only for a few. How does the country move forward from this state of apathy, where the hands of leaders are so immersed in the cookie jar, afraid that if they were to pull out, apartheid would return with vengeance? Perhaps the latter might be the answer to all of us who are lamenting the atrocities that are currently committed by those who initially professed to be the saviors only to become the villains.

The healing of this lovely country for those who were disenfranchised, exploited, lied to and who lost loved ones during the massacres of Sharpeville, the riots of 1976, 1985's state of emergency to name a few, is going to take a long time. Taking on the problems of other countries only exacerbates South Africa's situation especially when foreigners who were less valued in their own countries suddenly find themselves highly rated in South Africa as workers at the expense of the locals. I got to learn more about what seems to be the basis of the tensions and perhaps defensiveness between local Black South Africans and foreigners. This conversation which unfortunately, turned out to be uncomfortable took place on a trip to Cape Town during my last visit to South Africa. Out of curiosity to speak in my native tongue, I struck a conversation with an Uber driver who picked up my daughter, sister and I from the airport on our arrival to Cape Town. Obviously excited to be back home, I often strike up conversations with taxi, or Uber drivers expecting them to

172

indulge me in South Africa's dry humor. However, I came to realize that some were responding somewhat guarded and their responses were not in either of the common dialects Tsotsi tall, Xhosa or Zulu but in English. The first Uber driver I encountered had picked us up at the airport in Cape Town on our way to the hotel. After we were settled inside the car, I simply asked about the weather since it was overcast and somewhat gloomy. He kept on saying, 'Yes Madam.' I dismissed him as perhaps just polite. The second Uber driver took us from a Cape Town residence to the wineries in Stellenbosch. He was stocky built, feisty man with no sense of humor. I sensed he did not take kindly to any types of conversations with passengers but I was keen to engage him. Knowing that the Cape is Xhosa land, I engaged him in Xhosa and he simply ignored me. Then I followed up by asking if he spoke Xhosa or any of the other South African dialects. He quickly turned to face me as I was seated behind him simply stating, "No, Madame, I speak English." His demeanor was not friendly at all. At that point, my daughter sensing he was annoyed, nudged me to stop asking questions. I asked one more question and got a mouthful. By this time, I figured I had touched a nerve. He went on to tell me how he was recruited by the South African Soccer Association from his native country of Ghana to play for South Africa at the World Cup. After it was over, he chose to stay thinking there would be more opportunities for him to continue playing or coaching soccer. None of it happened. Instead he encountered xenophobic attitudes from South Africans. I shared with him how sorry I was to learn about his experiences, adding that Black South Africans are also hurting financially because of the scarcity of jobs. Unfortunately, he did not buy it, nor want to hear it. He went on to tell me I was wrong; I did not have my facts. He characterized Black South Africans as unprepared to work for what they considered to be low wages, in comparison to foreigners. He used himself as a good example.

He told me, the owner of the car he was driving was a Black South African who had previously hired another Black male South African to Uber for her. The arrangement did not work out after her car was abandoned at a Tavern. The driver and the money for that weekend were nowhere to be found. As a result, that was how he was hired as an Uber driver. The message to me was that to the employers of Uber drivers, hiring foreigners was less of a risk because they were honest and dependable compared to my fellow South Africans.

His message resonated with me throughout our stay in Stellenbosch. As I started interacting with hotel staff, restaurant servers and managers, I picked up on their accents and mannerisms. I realized all of them were foreign Blacks. I spent some time talking to a young server at one of the restaurants who told me he was recruited from a culinary school in Zimbabwe, acknowledging that almost all of them came from other African countries. He basically confirmed everything that was told to me by the Uber driver. Needless to say, I was hurt and disappointed that fellow South Africans who fought for equality and made sacrifices, yet here they were at a crossroads. Their leaders seemed to have completely forgotten about them. One cannot blame private businesses for doing what is in their best interest. The depth of South Africa's prevailing schism with politicians lacking a realistic vision for the country and the private sector trying to sustain the country's tourist industry, cannot be ignored. Greed has engulfed the public sector. Serving in the public sector appears to be the best route to enriching oneself at the expense of the populace, an irony to our ancestor's adage of Ubuntu which holds no meaning in today's South Africa.

Printed in the USA
CPSIA information can be obtained
at www.ICGtesting.com
LVHW051453220224
772305LV00053B/174

9 781804 393307